Bob Bondurant on
Race Kart Driving

Bob Bondurant and Ross Bentley

MBI Publishing Company

Special thanks to
Alan Rudolph, James Gue, and Jeff and Colin Braun
for their contributions to this book.

First published in 2002 by MBI Publishing Company, Galtier Plaza, Suite 200, 380 Jackson Street, St. Paul, MN 55101-3885 USA

MBI Publishing Company books are also available at discounts in bulk quantity for industrial or sales-promotional use. For details write to Special Sales Manager at Motorbooks International Wholesalers & Distributors, Galtier Plaza, Suite 200, 380 Jackson Street, St. Paul, MN 55101-3885 USA.

Library of Congress Cataloging-in-Publication Data Available
ISBN 0-7603-1076-9

Front cover photo: Mark LaCour, MLP Imaging

Back cover photo: Rick Scuteri

Interior photos: Rick Scuteri unless otherwise indicated

Cover design: James Tantillo and MBI Design Team

On the front cover: Driver Alan Rudolph at the 2001 Superfinals in Las Vegas.

Bob Bondurant is a former race champion and the founder of the Bob Bondurant School of High Performance Driving in Phoenix, Arizona, where he lives.

Ross Bentley is an experienced race car driver, coach, and author who has driven everything from stock production cars to super modifieds to Indy cars. He lives in White Rock, British Columbia, and drives a shifter kart in his spare time.

Edited by Chad Caruthers
Designed by Dan Perry

Printed in the United States of America

Contents

Foreword

Bob and I met shortly after he returned from Ferrari's 50th anniversary party in Maranello, Italy. While at the party, Bob had a chance to speak with Michael Schumacher, Ferrari's World F-1 Champion. During their conversation, Michael mentioned to Bob how important shifter karts were to his training routine.

Immediately upon Bob's return, he began inquiring about shifter karts. Bob got my name through a mutual acquaintance and contacted me with the idea of starting up a shifter kart school. He wanted to develop a shifter kart curriculum, which he would model after his world-renowned School of High Performance Driving. With this venture, he was looking for vehicle sponsorship.

Bob's interest in shifter karting presented a great opportunity for both shifter kart racing and our company. If kart racing needed just one thing, it was a higher level of awareness. You'd find it difficult to locate a driver on the Indy 500 grid who didn't get there through karting, yet no one knows about it.

Entering into a partnership with Bob Bondurant, who owns the highest-profile high-performance driving school in America, would allow karting to get the exposure it needed while also showcasing SSC's karts and chassis, which are manufactured by CRG, the largest kart chassis builder in the world.

Three and a half years later, the Bondurant SuperKart School is everything we knew it would be. As expected, Bob's team of professional kart instructors have mastered the high-quality standards, all of which are utilized in Bob's car school.

SSC/CRG looks forward to a long and mutually rewarding relationship with the *best* in the business.

–Joe Ramos
President, Karbz Inc., dba SSC Racing

1

Welcome to Karting

Kart racing is tremendous fun. It's great racing and a great way for young kids to learn concentration, desire, and self-control. It allows them to grow up to be very fine ladies and gentlemen. In addition, it allows them to grow up to be some of the best American race drivers we'll ever see. In Europe, almost all great race drivers today started out in kart racing at five to six years of age. By the time they're teenagers, they've run hundreds of races and have thousands of miles under their belts. The next American to become a Formula One (F1) driver will come from kart racing.

When I started racing motorcycles I was 15 years old. I raced dirt-track ovals when I was 18 and did quite well. All the motorcycle experience paid off in my car racing. Today, it's not racing motorcycles that pays off, it's kart racing. But the same type of feelings and experience are present. For instance, on motorcycles I was used to racing handlebar-to-handlebar and wheel-to-wheel. Kart racing is always that close.

I started racing cars when I was 22, and it was quite easy. I then had four wheels—I started out with a Morgan plus 4—so I also had fenders. Car racing came to me quite naturally. I raced here in the United States in Corvettes, Ferraris, *Old Yeller*, and other specials. Then I went to Europe in 1964 with Carroll Shelby and the Ford Cobras.

My first race was as co-driver with Phil Hill in the Targa Florio, which is 42 miles per lap with over 900 corners. We led until our axle broke. Two races later I was with Dan Gurney as co-driver at the Le Mans 24-hour race where we were first in class and fourth overall. We were the first GT car behind three Ferrari prototypes. Our mission was to beat the Ferrari GTOs in the World Manufacturers Championship. And Ferrari had never been beaten before. We missed by five points the first year. When we went back the second year we switched from the Cobra Roadsters to the Cobra Daytona Coupes. I won every race I ran, and we won the World Manufacturers Championship.

Welcome to the world of karting!

The following year I received a call from Mr. Ferrari. I had a personal meeting with him and decided to sign up with Ferrari. That's where I got my first Formula One ride, which was the last race of the season in 1965 at the U.S. Grand Prix. It was absolutely fantastic. After that, Ferrari decided to have an Italian driver for the 1966 season, so I drove the Ferrari prototypes. I drove a BRM Formula One car for most of 1966. During the last two races of the year I drove for Dan Gurney in the All American Racers Formula One car at the 1966 U.S. and Mexican Grands Prix.

The reason I bring this up is that my experience in motorcycles led me to win these races, because it was a natural feeling to have complete car feel and control. Racing motorcycles also gave me the mental self-control one must have to compete at the vehicle's and driver's limits. Today, it's all in karts.

Three and a half years ago I was invited by the president of Ferrari, Luca Montezemolo, to go over to Italy for their 50th anniversary. While I was there, I met Michael Schumacher. I had a nice conversation with him and asked why he was still racing shifter karts—if something were to happen while racing karts it could devastate his F1 career. Then he made a profound statement: "I continually practice in shifter karts simply to stay sharp. Shifter karts are the closest thing to an F1 car." I thought again about shifter

There's no better way to have fun or start a racing career than behind the wheel of a kart. Kart racing is enjoyed by thousands of people—children of all ages—throughout North America and the rest of the world. *GO Racing Magazine*

kart racing and realized that it's the closest thing to a Formula One car today. For a fraction of the cost, everything is quick and fast: steering, braking, acceleration, and handling. So this is how he stays in shape for Formula One.

I came back home and drove a shifter kart that belonged to one of my mechanics, and had an absolute ball. They are so much fun to drive—so fast, and their handling is fantastic. With their short wheelbase and wide track, they're nervous things to drive. I started taking lessons from other kart racers. I learned to drive the kart better, and I thought by teaching kids I could help bridge the gap between kart racing and car racing.

That was my main purpose for starting Bondurant SuperKart School.

Alan Rudolph, my chief instructor for the karting school, does a great job. He's won many, many kart races and championships. He also test-drives the Cobra Mustangs and the Formula Fords for me. All of this takes dedication, and Alan has no shortage of that, just as I am dedicated to my schools. His experience, and that of all my instructors, is one of the keys to the schools' success.

I put the SuperKart School together in the same fashion as I did with my Bondurant School of High Performance Driving. From the very beginning, I was committed to having the very best equipment. As it requires a great investment to develop and operate a school, I work with sponsors as much as possible. As with a professional race team, we promote our sponsors as much as they do us—it's a two-way street.

We use CRG karts for both our ProKarts and Shifters. Kawasaki is our sponsor for the six-speed, 35-horsepower, 125-cc racing engines. They are very reliable, very quick, and run great. The ProKarts run twin Briggs & Stratton motors—a popular class in Europe. There is no shifting in the ProKarts, and there's about 14 horsepower between the two motors. The ProKart is a great learning tool for people just starting in karts. It is very quick in handling, steering, and braking. It has rear brakes only, whereas the Shifter Karts have front and rear ventilated disc brakes. It's a very nice, easy way to learn. We also use ProKarts in our corporate team-building driving courses, where everyone participating gets to drive a kart as well as the Mustangs. They all love it because it's fun and they get to race for the first time and in a safe manner.

Kart racing is becoming more and more popular in North America, although we have a way to go to catch up to Europe and South America. That was another reason I wanted to start the karting school. I wanted to help promote this form of motorsport, and I want to help up-and-coming young racers succeed.

Why Karting?

It is generally accepted today that a young driver will have a very difficult time making it to the top in the auto racing world without having grown up behind the wheel of a kart. Karting has certainly produced many of the greatest drivers in the past 10 or 20 years. Emerson Fitipaldi, Ayrton Senna, Michael Andretti, Michael Schumacher, and just about every top young driver in open-wheel racing today learned the ropes behind the wheel of a kart.

Why is this the case? Why is karting almost a prerequisite to a career racing cars? There are many reasons, but the primary one is that anyone who has spent half a dozen or so years racing karts is going to have a huge advantage over another driver who did not. In his book *Why Michael Couldn't Hit,* in which he discusses why Michael Jordan struggle hitting baseballs so much he couldn't make the majors, Dr. Harold L. Klawans claims that an athlete's basic skills are developed before the age of 15. If these skills have not gone through the formation stages early in life, they will never reach their full potential.

Following this reasoning, the years that an under-15-year-old spends racing a kart develop the physical and mental programming that leads to the skills of a future racing champion. Does this mean that if you haven't raced karts from the age of 8 on, you will never become a CART or World Champion? It may be a little more difficult, but we have seen and trained many drivers who never sat in a kart until they were well beyond 15 who went on to become very successful. But kids who start karting at an early age definitely have an advantage because they have already developed their racing reflexes and mindset.

Of course, no amount of experience can replace one important key to success—desire. Whether racing karts or cars, all competitive drivers have desire—a desire to learn, a desire to improve, a desire to succeed. Without that desire, no amount of equipment, experience, or training will make you a champion.

At the Bondurant SuperKart School, or at any kart race anywhere in the world, we see all types of people: young, old, male, female, big, small. They may come here to learn to become the next world champion, or just to have fun.

From the first moment I drove a shifter kart, I knew I had to start the Bondurant SuperKart School. All karts are fun, challenging, and perfect training for other forms of racing.

However, most students at our school belong to one of three categories:

- They have set themselves a goal of someday driving Formula One, CART Champcar, or NASCAR, and want to learn everything they can to help them achieve that goal.
- They are currently racing karts, or are just thinking about beginning to race karts, and want to improve their abilities.
- They just want to experience the thrill of driving a kart.

The people in the first group believe karting is simply a means to an end, while the second group believes karting is an end in itself. In other words, karting is either the ideal place to learn the skills and techniques to move onto another form of motorsport, or a place to race and have fun throughout your life. It is not surprising to us how often people from the third group, after experiencing a kart, end up in one of the first two categories!

If you are reading this book, we suspect you fall into one of these three groups.

Why you choose to take up karting is really not that important, although it may help to determine how far you are willing to push things to learn a new technique, or how much of a risk you are willing to take to win a race or championship. If you are simply doing it to have fun, great! It is one of the most enjoyable sports you will ever find. But ask yourself what you expect to get out of karting, and be honest with your answer.

If you are doing it just for fun, it may be a bit much to expect to beat all the other drivers. After all, they may have only one thought in mind—to win every race and championship, and then move on to bigger things.

If you are taking up kart racing simply to improve your abilities when racing a car, be aware that there may be some techniques that are not all that important for you to use or learn. These techniques are those that definitely do not apply to car racing, such as leaning your body to change the weight distribution of the kart. On the other hand, if you intend to take up karting as a serious endeavor, then you are going to want to learn every little trick and technique you can.

As we mentioned earlier, kart racing attracts all types of people. For simplicity's sake, we have called the driver "he" in this book. In no way is this shorthand meant to imply that karting is for males only. Far from it! There are, and will continue to be, many very talented female racers with every bit as much ability and determination as their male competitors.

The bottom line when it comes to why a person should go kart racing is this: There is no other form of motorsport that provides the same level of fun at such a comparatively low cost.

Types of Karts

In the world of karting, there is a variety of different types and classes. There is road racing and there is oval-track racing. Within oval-track racing, there are paved ovals and dirt tracks. Road racing can actually be broken down into outdoor and indoor racing, as the latter has seen a real boom over the past few years—and the racing on the in-door tracks can be just as fierce as on the outdoor tracks.

Within road racing and oval-track racing, the karts are divided into a number of different

classes, depending on the age and experience of the driver; the engine type and size; whether the kart uses a centrifugal clutch, is direct-drive, or has a gearbox; or whether the driver lies down in the kart or sits up.

Basically, the engines are divided into four-stroke or two-stroke classes, and there are three basic systems by which the engine drives the rear axle:

- Clutch karts: These karts have an engine with a centrifugal clutch that engages and provides drive to the axle once it reaches a certain engine speed. The typical rental kart uses this drive system.
- Direct-drive karts: The engines on these karts drive the axle through a chain, and there is no form of clutch to disengage the engine drive from the axle. There is simply a sprocket on the engine and the rear axle, and the chain connects the two.
- Shifter karts: These karts use an engine (60, 80, 125, and 250 cc) and transmission unit from, or derived from, a motocross bike. Typically, these have a five- or six-speed gearbox.

It almost goes without saying that the driving technique you use is going to vary somewhat depending on the type of kart and track you are driving on. In this book, we are going to cover the driving techniques for at least the most popular types and classes of karts. If we don't differentiate between techniques, you can assume the technique applies equally to all types of karts. In other words, we will only point out a variation in technique when it is warranted.

When it comes time to choose what type of kart is right for you, keep in mind one key rule: Do not invest in a kart that will break down every other time you run it. It is far better to buy a kart that will be easy to main-

Alan Rudolph, chief instructor at the Bondurant SuperKart School, briefs students prior to heading out on the track. The school sees students of both genders, of all ages, and from throughout North America.

tain than to have the latest, most up-to-date model. If you take on a kart that you end up spending more time working on than driving, you are more likely to lose interest in it. And when you then decide to sell it, you will find that you lose a lot on your investment! You also don't need a brand-new kart, just one that is in good shape and that will run reliably.

If your goal is to race shifter karts, and you want to win at that level, your best approach is to spend at least a season racing a 100-cc clutch or direct-drive kart. Why?

Because it is hard enough learning all the basics such as the cornering line, being smooth, proper braking techniques, and race-craft in a non-shifter kart, without having to worry about doing that while dealing with twice the horsepower and having to make 15 or 20 gear changes every 30-second lap. For at least your first season, you should concentrate on learning the fundamentals of kart driving. Once you have learned these basics, you can then add the complexities of driving a shifter kart. Although this may not be what you

With large grids, the various classes of clutch karts provide tight competition. For years it has been the most popular type of kart in North America, whether road-course or oval-track racing. *GO Racing Magazine*

Direct-drive karts are the basis for the world championship and are especially popular in Europe. Most of today's Formula One drivers came up through the ranks by racing direct-drive karts. *Jeff Deskins-SwiftSport*

want to hear, if your goal is to be a great karter, it is imperative that you race a non-shifter kart first.

Your other main consideration in deciding what type of kart you should race is what class is popular in your area. We suspect your goal is to go racing, rather than just go out and drive around the track by yourself. In some areas of the country, certain classes do not have many participants. It is not difficult to choose a class of kart that has only a couple of karts in it, but that won't give you much competition. Go to the local kart events and make note of the classes with the larger fields. Talk to some of the drivers competing in that class. Try to determine if the participation in that class is growing or not. If you want to learn the most in the shortest amount of time—and have the most fun—look for a racing class that will pit you against a good crop of determined drivers.

Learning

No matter what your reason for taking up karting, one of your objectives should be to learn as much as possible in as short a period of time as possible. We hope that is why you are reading this book.

With that in mind, the first thing we want to do is ask you to keep an open mind about

By far the fastest-growing class of karting in North America is shifter karts. In terms of thrill-per-dollar, they can't be beat. They are also used extensively by CART, IRL, NASCAR, and F1 drivers to "stay in shape."

the skills and techniques we are going to present here. If you have been driving a car for a number of years, you may have some habits that are going to need to be changed. There may also be some things that may not seem right to you at first. Trust us, they work. If you use them and make them your habits, it will go a long way toward you becoming faster and a race winner. And if you are not driving a car yet, great! The habits you develop now will serve you well for a long time—in karts, in race cars, and when driving on the street.

Understand that the process of learning is not a steady upward curve. You will face some

plateaus along the way, points where it seems you are never going to improve. From our experience, it's when a driver has apparently reached a plateau, when he is about to make a big leap forward in his performance—that is, if the driver does not become frustrated by the seeming lack of progress and forget about the basic principles presented in this book.

Speaking of the basics, there is an important rule to keep in mind, particularly when it comes to learning how to drive the correct line through a corner. That rule is: if you can't do it right at low speed, you will never be able to do it at high speed. You need to make sure you are doing everything right at a moderate speed before trying to drive absolutely flat out. Get the technique right first, then work on picking up speed. In fact, in most cases, if you get the technique dead on and you work on being smooth, your speed will just naturally pick up without even trying. That is by far the best way of becoming quick.

Over the past 30 or so years at the Bondurant School, we have seen more than 80,000 drivers of all different levels. There have been times where a driver has struggled to get the hang of high-performance or race driving, and has then gone on to become a great racer. Other people who have appeared to have an abundance of natural talent the first time in a race car never seem to progress much past that point. The reason? The drivers who seem to have all this "natural talent" forget that no matter how good they are right now, they will always have to work at improving. They think they know it all, and have it all, and believe that is going to lead them to becoming the next world champion.

The drivers who go on to become champions have usually come back to the school a number of times, always with the attitude of wanting to learn more and improve. That may just be the number-one reason for them becoming champions. They are willing, in fact desperate, to learn more—to constantly improve.

The point is that it doesn't matter how much natural talent you have; you will always have to work at improving. If you don't seem to be getting it at the beginning, don't worry. If you persist, keeping the information suggested in this book in mind, you will succeed. And if you seem to have it all figured out from the very start, don't think it will always come that easily. You too will have to keep working on the basics if you want continued success.

Karts to Cars

If your objective in racing karts is ultimately to progress into racing cars, it is important to understand the similarities and differences between the two. This is one of the advantages of the Bondurant SuperKart School. As the only school that has a full range of car and kart driving courses, The School understands the unique aspects of each vehicle type and the relationship between the two.

As you would expect, there are a number of similarities between racing cars and karts. After all, they both have an engine and four tires! Number one is the concentration it takes to be successful. Then there is the sense and feel it takes to drive anything at the limit—fast! Part of that comes from using your vision appropriately—for example, looking far ahead. Also required is smooth accelerating, steering, and braking. Most of the techniques you will use in one form of racing will apply equally to the other.

Actually, in the beginning it may seem easier for many to drive a car than a kart. Most cars, especially production-based cars, are slower reacting in their handling. A Formula Ford, in fact, handles similar to a kart but may be easier to drive.

Many karts are quicker than race cars. Everything is a lot faster. They corner faster, accelerate faster, and stop faster. And a kart is built is just like a real race car. With a kart, you have to be right on top of it all the time.

Of the 150 vehicles at the Bondurant School, the shifter karts are the quickest. When a lot of regular students go through the four-day Grand Prix course or the three-day High Performance course, if they drive one of

An SVT Mustang, Formula Ford, and shifter kart—a full range of training vehicles at the Bondurant School. Guess which of these is the quickest? Fast things come in small packages.

our shifter karts the first or second day they are here, they will do much better in the Formula Fords. Definitely, if someone has driven a kart, he is going to be just that much better when he gets into a car.

Setting a kart up—adjusting and tuning the handling—is much different from doing so on a car. In fact, many times it seems to be the reverse of setting a car up. To someone with a car background, it can be confusing at first. The important thing is to understand

and use the theory and concepts of why a certain change affects a kart in such a way. With that knowledge in mind, it shouldn't be any more difficult to understand and use.

With that knowledge in hand, moving from karts to cars one day will not seem so confusing. The key is to understand the "why" behind a specific setup change, not just the "what"—understanding why a change affects a kart the way it does is far more important than knowing just what to change.

2
Kart Dynamics

If you made a list of every component on your kart—every nut, bolt, engine part, chassis part, wire, cable—and then prioritized them based on how each item contributed to your speed and consistency on the track, the first four items would be:

- Tire
- Tire
- Tire
- Tire

The fifth through last components on the list would include the chassis itself, the engine and exhaust system, and every other part. This is not to say all those other components are not important. They are. Obviously, it is the entire package that really determines the vehicle's performance potential. But the single most critical component is your tires, especially from the driver's perspective. Everything you do as a kart driver is communicated through the tires.

In other words, your tires are the greatest single contributor to your success behind the wheel. That does not mean that you necessarily have to have the latest and greatest,

most sticky, brand-spanking-new set of tires on your kart every time you head out on the track. What it does mean is that to be fast, to win kart races, you must know how to treat your tires, how to read your tires, and what they are trying to tell you. You need to understand tires.

Tire Traction—What Is It?

Throughout this book, and your driving career, you will hear a lot about tire traction. Although most of us have a pretty good idea of what traction is, let us explain it here so that we all are working from the same page.

Tire traction is based on a number of factors, including the coefficient of friction of the track surface (just how grippy the pavement is), the construction and rubber compound of the tire itself, and the loading, or weight pushing down on the tire.

For a demonstration of these factors, grab a couple of erasers, one hard and one soft. Take one of them and push it along a smooth surface, a desktop, noting how much force is required to move it. Then push the same

Kart dynamics to the extreme—in this case, a kart "bicycling" around a corner. *GO Racing Magazine*

eraser along an abrasive surface, such as a carpet or rough concrete sidewalk. This demonstrates the difference in the coefficient of friction of track surface.

To see the difference between rubber compounds, compare the force it takes to push the two erasers across the same surface. The softer one has more traction, right?

And finally, to note the effect load has on tire traction, push an eraser across the surface of a desk. Then, push down hard on the eraser—adding load or weight to it—and note how much more effort or force it takes to make it slide.

If you want to be a successful kart racer, get to know your tires. Understand the different types and compounds of tires, and what varying the tire pressures can do for you; also learn how to read what the tire surface wear is telling you.

The tires on a kart are the main suspension component, allowing the kart to follow variations and undulations in the track surface. Notice the flex in the right rear tire of this kart as it corners heavily.

Slip Angle

The term "slip" in "slip angle" is a little confusing, but the concept is not difficult to understand. While the term slip is not completely accurate, it will work for our purposes here. In order for tires to generate maximum grip, they must "slip" a little. When you turn the steering wheel, the front tires point at an angle away from the straight-ahead direction. A tiny fraction of a second after you turn the steering wheel, the kart changes direction.

But it doesn't go exactly where the front tires are pointing. Instead, it follows an arc slightly larger than the ones the front tires are pointing to—it doesn't turn as sharp. In other words, there is a difference between the direction the tires are pointing and the direction the kart is traveling. The angle formed by those two lines of direction is called the tire slip angle.

If that angle is zero, the kart is following exactly the direction the tires are pointing.

The key to quickness in a kart is keeping the tires at their limit of adhesion (traction) all the way through the braking zone, the corners, and while accelerating out of the turns.

That will only happen when the kart is being driven slowly. As your speed picks up and the tires begin to slide slightly, the slip angle increases. At some point, when the slip angle is between 6 and 10 degrees, the tires are generating their maximum amount of grip. If you exceed that range by driving even faster, the kart will slide more, and you will be beyond the tires' ideal slip angle range.

What this tells you is that if the kart is not sliding slightly through the corners, you are not driving fast enough; conversely, if it is sliding too much because you are trying to drive too fast, the tires will not be gripping the track as well as they could. If the kart ever—even for a fraction of a second—feels as though it is on rails, you are going too slow. If you are sliding through the corners in a big drift, you are scrubbing off speed.

The real challenge, of course, is knowing just how much tire slip is ideal, and how much is not enough or too much. The ability to sense

The big challenge in driving a kart is knowing just how much to slide through the turns. Too little, and you are not driving fast enough; too much, as in this photo, and you will scrub off speed. Balancing the kart and its tires at the very limit is what being quick is all about.

and feel this comes mostly from trial-and-error experience: pushing it a little beyond, dialing it back, going beyond, bringing it back—homing in on that ideal range where the kart is at the limit and you are fast.

It's worth mentioning that there is a special case where the kart should feel as though it is on rails, and that is with a low-power kart on a very grippy track—one with lots of traction. In this case, it is even possible for the kart to have too much traction. The problem is that all this traction "binds" the kart up, scrubbing off speed. This is one of those situations that is hard to describe, but the moment you experience it you will recognize it. Typically, your goal is then to reduce the amount of traction the kart has, to allow it to run free.

Tire Contact Patch

All you have connecting you to the track are four tire contact patches, the actual part of the tire at the bottom that is in direct contact with the track surface. These contact patches depend on the size of the tire and the weight distribution of the kart. Generally, keeping as much of these four contact patches on the road surface as possible as you go around the track will give you the most traction.

To understand contact patches and the weight distributed between them, let's take a look at a car for a moment. What happens when a driver mashes down on the throttle? In addition to the car accelerating away, its rear squats down. The laws of physics tell us this is caused by the mass of the car wanting to remain where it once was—an object at rest tends to remain at rest. This changes the weight distribution of the car. Where the car's weight might have been distributed equally front to rear (50 percent of the weight on the front tires, 50 percent on the rears) when sitting still, as the car accelerates, weight is transferred to the rear. Now, maybe as much as 75 percent of the car's weight is on the rear tires, and only 25 percent on the front. The total weight of the car has not changed, just the way it is distributed. The rear tires will develop increased traction and the front tires will experience a decrease in traction.

You may be thinking to yourself, that is fine for a car with its springs, shock absorbers, and suspension, but a kart does not have a suspension that can squat down under acceleration. It doesn't matter—the laws of physics still apply. It may be more difficult to see or even feel the weight transfer from the front to the rear under acceleration with a kart, but it is still happening. That is why most karts have larger tires on the rear than they do on the front—because they have to corner and accelerate, while the fronts only have to corner.

The same thing occurs during braking, only in the opposite direction. Again, think about a car. When the driver applies the brakes, the car nose-dives, transferring weight onto the front tires. That is why cars have larger brakes on the front than they do on the rear—because the fronts are doing most of the braking work. And, even though many karts have brakes only on the rear, still the laws of physics demand that weight will transfer forward when braking, or even just lifting off the throttle.

And if this weight transfer works fore and aft (longitudinally), it surely must work from side to side (laterally) while cornering. When going around a right-hand corner, for example,

weight transfers toward the outside, taking load away from the tires on the inside of the turn (the tires on the right side of the kart) and placing more load on the outside tires (the left-side tires).

As you increase the weight on a tire, its contact patch gets larger, providing more grip. Picking up one of those rubber erasers again, put a lot of weight on it and notice how it squishes, and how the area in contact with the desk or table increases. The same thing applies to tires. If you increase the amount of weight on a tire, the size of the contact patch increases, and the tire gains traction. Not surprisingly, the opposite holds true as well. Reduce the weight on a tire, and the size of the contact patch gets smaller, and the traction level decreases.

Keeping in mind how this weight transfer works, and the fact that a tire with more load on it has more grip, you can begin to understand how your driving can affect how a kart handles. If, while driving through a turn, you put more load on the front tires by lifting off the throttle, the front tires will have more grip than the rears, possibly resulting in the rear of the kart beginning to slide. Or, if you accelerate hard in the middle of a turn, the weight will shift to the rear, unloading the fronts and loading the rears. This will result in the front tires beginning to slide.

As you can see, your driving technique affects the balance of the kart, which in turn affects the handling characteristics—understeer or oversteer.

Understeer and Oversteer

Understeer and oversteer are two terms anyone around racing for any length of time will hear. Let's look at them closely now to understand them fully.

Understeer occurs when the front tires have less grip than the rear tires do when

When a kart is understeering, the front tires are sliding more than the rear tires, and the kart tends to plough straight ahead.

going around a corner. As you turn the steering wheel, asking the front tires to change the direction of the kart, the rear tires—having more grip than the fronts—win the battle and drive the kart near straight ahead. The kart is now "pushing," or following a path of a larger radius than you had intended. In other words, the kart has not *steered* or turned as much as you would have liked, so it has understeered.

Oversteer is the opposite. The rear tires now have less grip than the front tires do when going around a corner. As you turn the steering wheel, the front tires—having more grip than the rears—change the direction of the kart, and the rear tires begin to slide sideways. The kart is now "loose," meaning the kart is following a

path tighter than you had intended. In other words, the kart has steered more than you had wanted, so it has oversteered.

Another term not as often heard is neutral steer. As the name implies, the kart is neither understeering nor oversteering, but is in a neutral state with all four tires sliding an equal amount. At first thought, you may conclude this is the ideal handling state, and you may be right most times. However, there are times when you want the kart to either understeer or oversteer—times when one or the other of these two handling states will make you get through a turn faster.

For example, in a tight hairpin turn, having a kart that oversteers will often help you

When the rear tires are sliding sideways more than the front tires, that's oversteer. It may look great—and it's lots of fun—but too much oversteer means you will be slow. Your goal is to find that perfect balance between understeer and oversteer: neutral steer.

get it rotated around the corner quicker, enabling you to begin accelerating sooner. Or, in a very fast sweeping turn where it would be difficult and maybe even dangerous to have an oversteering kart, a slight amount of understeer may be ideal.

What causes a kart to understeer or oversteer? One or a combination of two things: the chassis setup and your driving technique. We'll get into chassis setup in chapter 9; for now, let's focus on your driving.

Making Tires Work for You

Remember the rubber erasers you were pushing across a table? When you put more load on one of them by pressing down, it

gripped the table more. The same thing applies to your kart tires. If your driving causes more weight or load to be put on the front tires, they will have more grip or traction than the rears, and vice versa.

When many drivers start to get into a slide in a corner, they lift off the gas pedal, maybe even jump on the brakes, and they spin. This is because the driver's abrupt inputs caused weight to shift forward suddenly—the rear tire contact patch got smaller, and the front tire patch got bigger. In addition, the back end came around because front traction overpowered traction at the rear.

As you drive and the kart passes over the road, the four tire contact patches transmit a

Much of the ability to sense when the tires are at their limit comes from the feedback your hands receive through the steering wheel. If you are holding the wheel with a death grip, you will miss out on some of the feedback. Concentrate on relaxing your arms and hands.

message about their relationship to the track. This message travels from the tire to the chassis, chassis to the steering column, steering column to the steering wheel, through the steering wheel hub, up the spokes, and around the rim. From there, that information is transmitted through your hands, up your arms, and to your brain. Your brain then makes decisions and/or directs your body to do something based on that information.

Your brain also receives information from other parts of your body in contact with the chassis. You sense and feel from the balls of your feet on the pedals; heels on the floor; the bottom of your legs and buttocks on the seat; lower, middle, and upper back; shoulders in the seat, and the palms of your hands; and fingers on the steering wheel. Anything that is in direct contact with the kart provides feedback from the tires.

This feedback from the tires, through the kart chassis to your body, only gets transmitted to your brain if the muscles in your body are relaxed. If they are tense, the feedback is restricted—only a limited amount of information from the tires will get to your brain. Your sense and feel of what the kart is doing will be reduced.

Think of the tires on your kart as your friend. They help you. They give you a lot of information that you can use to help you go faster. They tell you whether you are driving at the limit of traction or not. If you are not at the limit of traction, you are not driving fast enough. You have to listen to your tires. You have to treat them with respect, by not doing anything abrupt to them, or by asking too much from them.

You can sense and feel what the tires are doing, your body can sense and feel every move the kart makes, and you can tell when your tires are working or not working. In fact, if you change the tires' pressures by even one-half a pound, you should be able to notice whether the kart has more or less traction. You must be sensitive to what your friends, the tires, are telling you.

In a kart, as in any vehicle, you can do three things: accelerate, brake, or steer. Every time you turn the steering wheel, you are asking the tires to do something for you. Every time you brake, you are asking the tires to do something for you. Every time you accelerate, you are asking the tires to do something for you. And if you happen to do two of those things at once (turn the steering wheel and accelerate at the same time, for example), you are asking your tires to do an awful lot for you!

Having said that, you can brake, corner, or accelerate separately, or you can combine two or even all three at the same time. In fact, to drive a kart as fast as it can possibly go—right at the very limit—you must overlap or combine braking, cornering, and/or acceleration in varying degrees. Why? And what determines to what degree you overlap them? Your tires will tell you.

The four tires on your kart have a specific and limited amount of traction, or grip. You can use all of the tires' traction, 100 percent of it, for braking. You can use 100 percent of it for cornering. You can use 100 percent of it for accelerating. Or, you can use 100 percent of it for a combination of these three forces. But you can't get more than 100 percent from them.

For example, on the approach to a turn, you can use 100 percent of the tires' traction for braking. Then, as you get to the point where you need to turn the steering wheel and begin to use some traction for cornering, you need to ease off the brakes a little—let's say you are using 10 percent of traction for cornering and 90 percent for braking. As you go farther into the turn, you continue to turn the steering wheel more—using more traction for cornering—and continue to ease off the brakes. In other words, you are trading some braking traction for cornering traction. Eventually, you will have come off the brakes entirely (0 percent braking), at which point you are at maximum cornering (100 percent cornering). Then, as you pass the apex of the turn, you begin to unwind (straighten) the steering wheel, giving up some cornering traction for acceleration traction (90 percent cornering, 10 percent acceleration; 50 percent cornering, 50 percent acceleration; 25 percent cornering, 75 percent acceleration, and so on).

As you can see, there is an overlap, or combination, of the three forces. But—and this is absolutely critical—you cannot get more than 100 percent out of the tires. For example, you cannot expect to use even 1 percent of the

Surprisingly, a lot of your speed does not come from your right foot on the throttle; it comes from knowing when and how to squeeze the brakes on, and when and how to ease off. Developing a sensitive left foot is critical to being fast in a kart. That is one of the reasons karters do so well in Formula One and Champ cars, as left-foot braking is the way to be fast in them as well.

tires' traction for braking while cornering at 100 percent, without the kart sliding or spinning out of control. This technique of entering the turn while easing off the brakes—still braking while turning into the corner—is called trail braking. It is the only way to use all of the tires' traction, and to go really fast in a kart (or car, for that matter). We will discuss trail braking more in chapter 5.

Again, the important thing to understand is that to drive at the very limit, you must use all 100 percent of the tires' traction at all times—but never exceed it. That is where the challenge and thrill of driving at the limit comes from. If you don't totally understand what we've just talked about, go back and reread it over and over again until it makes perfect sense to you.

3
The Basics

Just getting in and out of a kart for the first time can be a project all its own. If you want to look as though you know what you are doing with a kart, then you will want to use the right technique. Start by simply stepping onto the seat itself, squat down, place both of your hands on the upper back edge of the seat, and step your feet forward to the gas and brake pedals. (Avoid stepping on the steering arms—they will bend.) Then, lower yourself down until you are sitting on the front edge of the seat.

One of the first things you will notice about kart seats when you look at them is that they are more narrow in the area that surrounds your ribs than they are in the area around your buttocks. That should tell you something about getting in and out of the seat: if you try to squeeze your buttocks straight down into the seat, it will be tough going. If you sit down on the front edge of the seat and then slide back into the seat, it will be much easier. Just reverse this process to get out of the kart.

One last thing about getting in and out.

Always step in and out of the kart from the side opposite the engine. This side is much easier and you are less likely to burn yourself on a hot engine or exhaust pipe.

Once you are in the seat, your positioning is very important. If the seat is tilted back too far, you can't sense and feel the kart as well. If you sit up straight, the feedback from the kart starts at the base of your spine and travels up

Learning the basics is not just important, it's critical. Without the basics you will never be able to learn the more advanced techniques, and you will never reach your potential.

If you want to look like a pro, learn how to how to get in your kart like a pro. Step onto the seat, support and then lower your body onto the front of the seat with both arms—while slipping your feet onto the pedals—and then push your buttocks back into the seat.

your back to your neck and, along with your eyes, feeds information to your brain. But if you are slouched, the energy doesn't travel up your back as fast. When you're upright you get the energy directly from your buttocks to your brain, telling you what's going on. If you are sitting, even at a desk or in a chair in a seminar, sit up straight with your feet on the ground. When you sit up straight you're going to have more sense and feel, and you'll be more alert.

Having said that, how far your seat is tilted back has an effect on the handling of the kart. If the kart oversteers too much, one of the ways to improve that is by adjusting the seating position. By tilting the seat back farther, so that when you're going through a corner, your body weight is going over and pushing more weight on the outside rear tire. So even though it is best to be seated as upright as possible, there are times when you have to compromise your position to suit the kart's chassis setup. But do

Here's a driver comfortably seated behind the wheel, ready to drive. When you're sitting in the proper position, you receive more feedback from the kart.

keep in mind that even if you make the kart have more rear traction by tilting the seat back, if you can't feel it due to the odd seating position, you won't be very fast.

When you are sitting in the kart, you should always have a slight bend in your arms at the elbows, even when your hand is at the top of the steering wheel (at the 12 o'clock position). You should not have to stretch, or even fully straighten your arms to reach the top of the steering wheel.

The best hand position for the steering wheel in a car is at 3 and 9 o'clock, contrary to what you may have been taught in driver's ed. In a kart it is best to move them up to around 2 and 10 o'clock. The reason for this has to do with the weight transfer we talked about earlier. Imagine turning into a left-hand corner. With your hands beginning at the 10 and 2 position, and your right hand pushing up on the steering wheel, it will actually put a load onto the top of the steering wheel as you go around the corner. Never shuffle or reposition your hands on the wheel. Hold the wheel at 10 and 2 and don't move your hands from that position—keeping them there offers the most control, accuracy, and smoothness, and loads the outside front tire in a corner: the load on the steering wheel transfers down the steering column to the outside front tire, giving it more grip.

It is very important that you stay relaxed behind the wheel. When you tighten up— when you tense up the muscles in your arms

Notice how this driver has a slight bend in both arms, allowing him to control the steering wheel precisely, quickly, and smoothly. If your arms are stretched straight out reaching for the wheel, you will tire quickly and have less control.

and shoulders, for example—you lose some of the sense and feel for what the kart is doing. Your body is very smart. If you're going too fast for your comfort level, your body will start to tighten up. It's telling you, "Slow down." And if you don't listen, then you get jerky and you can lose control. When you tighten up, you can easily lose 50 percent of the sense and feel and control of the kart.

As a demonstration of this, as you drive down the highway in a car, grip the steering wheel very tightly. Notice how much vibration and feedback you feel through the steering wheel. Then, relax your grip on the wheel, holding it with a light grip of your fingers. Note the vibration and feedback now. Much more feedback with the relaxed grip, right?

The ideal position for holding the steering wheel is with the hands at the 10 and 2 o'clock position. You should never have to move your hands from this position to make any turn. If you have to move your hands to turn the steering wheel any more than this, you've made a big error!

The first time you drive a kart, it is likely you will hold the steering wheel with a "death grip." You will probably do less than a dozen laps before your arms are tired. That's because your arms are tense. You may have to make a conscious effort to relax your arms and grip on the wheel. After you have driven a kart for a while, you will naturally begin to feel more relaxed. As your arms relax, you will receive more feedback through the wheel. That is much of the feedback you use to sense and feel when the kart is at the limit through the corners.

Driving a kart fast is not about how you manhandle it. Unfortunately, you do hear a lot of talk about how sometimes you just have to get after the kart—grab it by the scruff of the neck and go after it. You still need to do that with finesse, though. It's what we call "aggressively smooth."

Physical Fitness

Driving a kart is far more physically demanding than most people would imagine. To be good at kart racing, it takes strength and stamina, two things that will not come about just from racing even 15 or 20 times a year. If you want to be successful in racing, you are going to have to work at getting in shape for it. After all, it is a sport just like any other. In fact, it is physically more demanding than many other sports.

Therefore, you owe it to yourself to do some training. If you are racing simply for fun, you don't have to go overboard with your training. But the more fit you are, the more fun it will be. After all, how much fun can it be to be out of breath and have most of your muscles aching at the halfway point of a race?

If you are looking at karting as a career or steppingstone to a career in car racing, your

You can always spot an out-of-shape driver near the end of a race, both by his performance and body position. This driver is having a difficult time holding his head upright. If your neck or any other part of your body is tired and sore after a race, you need to do some physical training.

training had better be more than just something you do in your spare time. It must be a planned-out aspect of your preparation, just like having your kart's engine rebuilt and chassis aligned.

So what kind of training is required? Stamina is more important than outright strength, as it does not take a huge amount of effort simply to turn the steering wheel, press the pedals, and support your body while zipping around the turns for a lap. A few laps at speed, though, and just holding your head upright with the weight of a helmet on it becomes a chore. That's why you need to work on your physical stamina.

A regular routine of lifting weights and developing your cardiovascular endurance (through running, Stairmaster, cycling, and so on) is required to achieve your highest potential. The key word is "regular." Training every day for one week, and then not training for another month, is not going to be very effective. You would be better off training two days a week, every week. And, as we said, relying on the workout you receive from racing alone will not be enough. At that rate, you will probably stay at the level of just getting tired near the end of a race. The last time we looked, every race is decided on the last lap, no matter how big a lead a driver has.

Your goal is to be able to drive every lap of practice, qualifying, and the race(s) at an event, and still be able to drive one more session without tiring. If you are worn out by the end of a race event, your performance will have suffered because before you notice yourself being tired or hurting, you will have been compensating subconsciously for the tired and sore muscles. Any time you have to compensate, you will not perform as well as you could.

Weight

Your physical weight has a great effect on the performance of both you and your kart.

Racing karts weigh in the vicinity of 260 to 400 pounds including the driver, with engines producing between 6 and 42 horsepower. When you calculate the total power-to-weight ratio, you begin to understand just why karts are so fast. The other thing that becomes apparent is just how much your own weight factors into the equation—far more so than with any race car.

For example, let's look at a 100-cc direct-drive kart, piloted by a 140-pound driver. For that class of racing, most rule books say the kart and driver must weigh a total of 280 pounds. That means the kart itself must weigh in at 140 pounds, even if that means adding ballast to it. A typical 100-cc Yamaha engine puts out around 22 horsepower, resulting in a power-to-weight ratio of 0.079 horsepower per pound. Now, let's say the driver happens to put on an extra 5 pounds in the off-season—the power-to-weight ratio changes to 0.077 to 1. That may not sound like much of a difference, but it is a 2.5 percent change, and a 2.5 percent change in lap time is an eternity in kart racing. That's equal to three-quarters of a second on a 30-second lap!

Here's another way of looking at this: a kart driver putting on 5 pounds is equal to a NASCAR Winston Cup driver putting on 63 pounds!

A kart and driver combination that is even one pound overweight takes longer to accelerate and to brake. In other words, it hurts in every way possible.

In addition, one of the most effective ways of adjusting the handling of your kart is by shifting the kart's weight distribution around. For example, you can do this by raising or lowering the seat, or moving it forward

Even though karts accelerate quickly, momentum is the key to being fast. Every time you slow them down, their little engines have to work very hard to accelerate the weight of the kart and driver back up to speed.

or backward. If you are light enough, you can also do that by altering where you place the ballast it takes to get you and your kart up to the required weight limit. The lighter you are, the more options you have. If you and your kart's total weight is right at the limit, and you are up against another driver who weighs 10 or 20 pounds less, who do you suppose is going to have the most options when it comes to fine-tuning the kart's handling by moving the ballast around? Right, your competitor.

Reducing your weight has another benefit other than how it affects your kart's performance. Fat on your body acts as insulation, meaning that any heat you have in your body will be more likely to stay in your body. If you can't dissipate heat well, the chances of your body overheating increase. When you overheat, you lose more body fluid (water), which hurts your performance both physically and mentally.

The point is, of course, if you want to be successful in kart racing, you are going to need to keep an eye on your weight. If you were born to be tall or heavy, the sooner you learn everything you can from karting and then move into racing cars (if that's your intention), the better—at least from a competitive standpoint. A 5, or even 10 or 20, pound disadvantage in the lightest of race cars will not create nearly as big a problem.

Diet

Having gone through the exercise of seeing how big a disadvantage weight is in karting, it's probably time to mention your diet. It goes without saying that anything you can do to keep your weight down will be a big benefit in racing karts. As we just saw, even if the total weight for you and your kart is not over the class weight limit, trimming weight off yourself will allow you better chassis tuning options because you can add ballast where you want to.

Most people know what types of foods can lead to weight gains and losses. Most people also know that certain foods will physically hurt their performance; some foods will make them more lethargic, affect their stamina, and zap their strength.

What most people don't know is how certain foods can hurt their mental performance. It is a fact that some foods slow your mental processing speed, which is obviously not a good thing when you are driving something as quick as a racing kart. The interesting thing is why these foods affect your mental performance. Yes, the actual makeup of the food—the amount of fat, the lack of nutrients, the inclusion of certain chemicals, and so on—has an effect on the chemicals in your brain. But even your beliefs about the food can affect your performance.

For example, if you firmly believe that a specific food is bad for you, that it will hurt your physical performance, and you eat it, your brain will tend to "switch off." That is, your negative beliefs about the food will cause your mental performance to suffer.

So, it is a double, and maybe even triple, whammy. Not only will a greasy hamburger hurt your physical performance, it will cause your brain's processing speed to slow down physiologically (from the lack of proper nutrients) and psychologically (from your beliefs about it).

What does this all mean? It means that if you are serious about being successful and having the most fun in your kart racing, you owe it to yourself to watch what you eat. There are dozens and dozens of books on the market that claim to have the ultimate diet. Most of these books are geared toward losing weight. If that's your only goal, find one that makes sense to you—and one that's practical for you—and stick to it.

But beware of weight-loss diets that do not provide the nutrition and energy that you will require to race. As we said, karting is hard work; it requires a lot of strength and stamina. Your body and mind are like an engine. If you do not provide enough fuel for an engine, it will not perform well. If you give it low-grade fuel, it will not perform well. Likewise, if you don't feed your body and mind enough, or give it high-quality fuel (food), it will not perform well.

Therefore, you may want to follow one of the diets geared more toward high-performance athletes, or meet with and follow the guidelines of a sports nutritionist. Then pay attention to how you perform after a meal. If you feel lethargic or mentally slow after a certain type of food, stay away from it. After doing this for some time, you will naturally crave the types of foods that lead you to great performances.

One last comment on your diet. Yes, what you eat on a race day or weekend is critical. However, if you have subsisted on junk food all week prior to an event, all the healthy food in the world is not going to make up for it on the race weekend.

4

The Art of Cornering

Driving in a straight line in a kart is a relatively simple thing to do. But the corner—that's where the real challenge and fun come in. In this chapter, you will learn about the cornering line—that almost mystical element many race drivers talk so much about. The goal is for you to understand the concepts of cornering so that you will be able to determine for yourself exactly what is the perfect, fastest line through each corner you face.

Corner Radius = Speed x Traction

Which is easier, driving in a straight line or going around a corner? Which can you go the fastest in? Driving straight, right? That should give you a clue as to the main theme behind how to drive through the corners: the straighter you can drive, the easier it will be and the faster you can drive.

The way to do that is drive the kart along a line or path through the corners with as large a radius as possible. In other words, straighten the corners as much as possible.

Let's try a little experiment. Tie a small weight (a couple of washers, for example) onto a piece of string about 2 feet long, and then twirl them around your head in a circle while holding the end of the string. Note the speed and the centrifugal force pulling outward on the weight.

Take that same weight and tie it to a piece of string about 6 feet long and do the same thing. You will notice that when you are twirling the weight on the end of the 6-foot string, the weight travels much faster with the same centrifugal force.

Now, imagine your kart as this weight, going around two corners, one with a 2-foot radius and the other with a 6-foot radius. Just like the weight on the end of a string, when the kart follows a larger radius, it can be driven faster.

Reference Points

Before we go any further, any discussion of the cornering line should begin by defining the reference points that you use to help guide you through a corner. There are three key reference points: turn-in, apex, and exit. When you combine that with a braking point on the approach to the corner, at first it becomes as simple as connecting the dots. Of course, you

Hustling a cart through a corner—one of the great reasons to go karting!

Driving a kart at the limit, on the perfect line through a corner, is one of the most enjoyable challenges you will ever face. Finding the ideal line is not as difficult as many drivers make it out to be.

Here's a kart at the turn-in point, about to initiate a turn into the corner from the outside edge of the track. If you get your turn-in right, the rest of the corner pretty much takes care of itself. So make sure you have an easy-to-recognize reference point.

Use every inch of track at the exit of the turns. As a general rule, the more track you use, the sooner you will be able to steer straight. And the sooner you steer straight, the sooner you can accelerate out of the corner.

Shown here is a kart at the apex area of a turn, against the inside edge of the track. Where you apex will determine how soon you can begin to accelerate and where you will exit.

will never be fast if you drive from point to point. No, it must be a flowing path, passing through these points.

Turn-In

The turn-in point is just as the name implies: the point where you begin to turn the steering wheel to follow a line through the corner. In most cases, where and how quickly you turn-in is going to dictate the line or path you follow through the rest of the corner—it will determine where you apex and exit the corner.

Apex

Often the apex is not one single point in a corner, it is an apex area. It is the area in the corner where you are clipping past the inside edge of the track. It is sometimes thought of as that point where you go from entering into the corner to exiting the corner.

The apex area may be a single point, a couple of inches long, where you clip past the inside edge of the track, or it may be many feet long where you follow the inside radius of the corner.

Exit

The exit point, sometimes referred to the track-out point, is the place on the track where you have let the kart run to the outside edge of the track surface. The key here is to

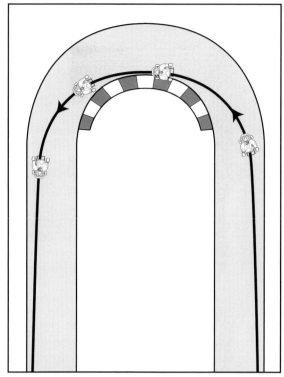

The geometric line from the outside edge of the track at the turn-in point, to the apex area on the inside edge of the track, and finally to the exit point at the outside edge of the track, is the fastest way to get through that individual turn, but it is not necessarily the fastest way to get around the entire race track.

exit, that when tied together in an arc result in the largest possible radius through the corner. This line, often referred to as the geometric line, is the fastest line to follow through the corner. When driving on a race track, however, you also have to consider the straightaways connecting the turns. In fact, even though the corners are more of a challenge, the straightaways may be more important. Why? First, on most tracks you will spend more time on the straightaways than you will in the corners, which means there is more time to gain or lose here. Second, the straightaways are where you will be traveling the fastest, which means there is more to gain or lose. And finally, it is much easier to pass your competitors on the straights than in the corners.

So, if the main theme behind the geometric line is simply getting through each individual corner as fast as possible, then the theme of the ideal line is to drive the corners in such a way that you will be fast through the corner and down the following straightaway.

To do that—to maximize your straightaway speed as well as your corner speed—you often have to alter your line from the

use all the track surface, which means the exit point will usually be at the outside edge of the track—this helps to increase the radius of the turn, "straightening" the turn more than if you stayed toward the middle or inside edge of the track.

Ideal Line

With the information you now have, you would think that determining the ideal line—the line that will result in the overall fastest lap time—through any corner would be simple. Just pick three points, the turn-in, apex, and

In a corner that leads onto a long straightaway, your objective is to drive a line through the corner that allows you to begin accelerating as early as possible. That means a late turn-in, apex, and exit.

geometric line. In other words, simply driving the line with the largest possible radius may not be enough.

The real challenge is determining just how much you need to alter your line from the geometric line. Too close to the geometric line, and you will be fast through the corner, but not fast down the straightaways. Altered too much and you will have good acceleration down the straightaway, but lose more than you gained because of how much more you have to slow down in the beginning of the corner. There is a balance between the two extremes, and that is the ideal line.

That is one of the main reasons for practicing: altering your line slightly to determine what is the ideal line for you and your kart in each corner.

Types of Corners

To find the ideal line, you must first determine what type of corner it is. Is it a corner that leads onto a straightaway, is it one that is at the end of a straightaway, or one that simply connects two other corners? Of course, there are corners that fit more than one of these categories. But, in most cases, the corner leading onto the straight is the most important, so it takes priority over any other type. The corner at the end of the straight is the second most important corner, so it takes priority over the third type: corners connecting corners.

Let's take a more detailed look at each of these types of corners.

Corners Leading onto Straightaways

When dealing with any corner that leads onto a straightaway, your main objective is to maximize the acceleration onto the straight. In fact, your acceleration onto the straight is more important than your speed through the corner.

The line you drive will determine the speed and amount of acceleration onto the straight. Instead of simply driving as large a radius as possible, your turn-in point should be slightly later, and the apex area approximately

When dealing with a series of turns, your main goal is to accelerate quickly out of the last corner and onto the straightaway. Typically, this means taking a late apex so that you are set up on the ideal line for the last corner in the series.

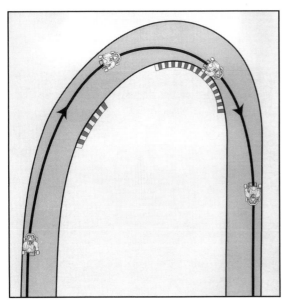

This illustration shows the ideal line for a decreasing radius corner. Notice the late apex, allowing room for accelerating onto the straightaway.

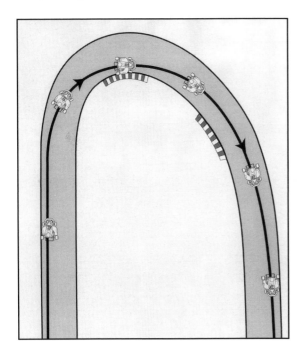

Here we see the ideal line for an increasing radius corner. Because of the increasing amount of track toward the exit, you should use a relatively early apex.

two-thirds of the way through the corner. That way, you will end up making a slightly tighter radius turn from the turn-in point to the apex, but from there the radius will be expanding. The expanding radius is the real key—it allows you to accelerate early and hard.

Recall our earlier discussion about how you can only get 100 percent of traction from a tire. If you are driving through a corner on the geometric line, with the tires at their cornering traction limit, when can you begin to accelerate? Not until you are at, or near, the exit point and you begin to straighten the steering wheel. But if you turn-in later, and head for a later apex, you will be able to begin accelerating as soon as you start to unwind (straighten) the steering. This will probably be before or at the apex of the corner, which is much sooner than if you had driven the geometric line.

You may have noticed, though, that to drive this ideal, later turn-in and apex line, you will have to slow down a bit more to make the initial tighter radius early in the corner. The fact that you can begin to accelerate earlier outweighs this one downside. You will easily compensate for the slower speed early in the corner by your increased speed out of the corner and down the straight. The rule in this type of turn is simple: slow in, fast out (of course, you don't want to go slower than you have to, just slow enough to hold the ideal line and blast out of the turn and down the straight).

Corners at the End of Straightaways

When you are faced with a corner at the end of a straightaway that does not then lead into another straightaway of reasonable length, your prime objective is to maintain your straightaway speed for as long as possible. So what defines a straightaway of reasonable length? That's difficult to say exactly, but generally it is any one in which there is not enough length for you to make a pass on another competitor.

To take full advantage of this type of corner, you want to carry as much speed into the turn as you can, even if that compromises your speed exiting it. To do that, you want to turn into the corner earlier than the geometric line, heading in as straight a line as possible toward an early apex. The key is to brake as late as possible for these corners, maintaining your straightaway speed for as long as possible. That means braking deep into the corner.

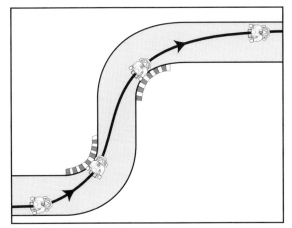

This illustration shows the ideal line for an "esse" bend. Notice the late apexes in each turn, which maximizes the acceleration out of the last turn and onto the straightaway.

This driver has straightened out the line through these esses and has the kart set up well for the acceleration onto the straightaway. The driver that finds the best series of compromises in a combination of turns will be the quickest.

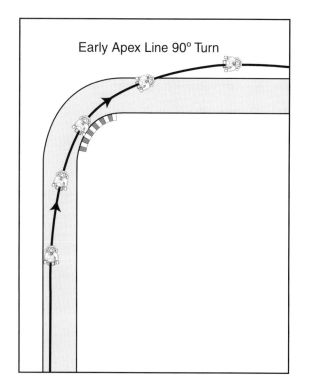

Early Apex Line 90° Turn

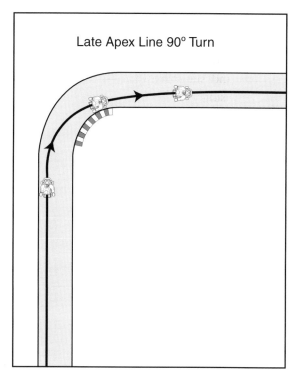

Late Apex Line 90° Turn

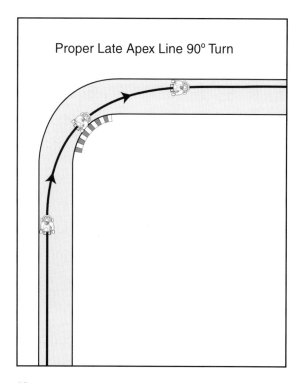

Proper Late Apex Line 90° Turn

Corners Connecting Corners

Most of the race tracks you will race your kart on have corners that do not lead onto a straight, nor are they at the end of one—they are between or connect other corners that are before and after straightaways.

Your goal for these corners is to get into position for the ensuing turn that ultimately leads onto a straightaway. That means doing whatever is necessary—compromising— to set up for that final corner in this combination of turns. The most important thing to keep in mind is your acceleration out of the last turn in the series.

Cornering Compromises

Being a great kart racer requires more than just being able to drive through one corner faster than everyone else. It demands being faster than everyone else around the entire track, and positioning your kart in such a way as to improve your chances of getting into the lead and staying there. That often means compromising your line in one area of the track to improve your performance in another.

It is very rare indeed that you will not have to compromise your line through one corner to set up for another. Most road-racing tacks have corners that link together, or where the exit of one corner sets you up on the wrong side of the track for the next one. A good rule of thumb is to compromise the earlier corner for the last one that leads onto a straightaway.

For example, the exit of a right-hand turn places you on the left-hand edge of the track. If this right-hander is followed closely by a left-hander that leads onto a straightaway, it is best to compromise the line through the first corner. It would be best to exit the right-hander more toward the middle or right side of the track so that the entry to the left-hander allows you to carry momentum into the turn and accelerate early. In other words, you give up some speed in the first corner to maximize your speed through the second corner and out onto the straightaway.

And remember, the fastest line around the race track may result in a quick lap time, but you may get passed by every other kart on the track. Why? Because the fast line often gives your competitors lots of room to make a pass. That means that the fastest line may not be your best racing line. We will talk more about this in chapter 6, but your racing line is certainly a case of compromise.

Momentum and the Line

You need to understand something else about the best line around the track: the perfect line for one kart and driver may not be the perfect line for another. There are some significant differences in lines for different types of karts. As a general rule, anything you can do to maintain your kart's speed and momentum is good. If that means driving a line through a corner that results in traveling a longer distance, often that is the way to go. Always remember: momentum is everything.

Having said that, momentum is less important in some karts than others. For example, it is not as critical with a shifter kart, for the very reason that you can usually just shift it down a gear to keep the engine in the ideal rev range for accelerating out of the corner. Obviously, with a direct-drive kart you cannot do that. Every time you slow a direct-drive down, it takes a lot of effort to get it going again. For that reason, if you can take a larger radius line through the corner that allows you to maintain the kart's speed, you will be faster coming out of the turn—even though you had to drive a greater distance to do it.

With a shifter kart, you can use more of a "point and shoot" style of driving, where you drive the kart into the corner, slow it down while knocking it down into the right gear, rotate it toward the apex, and stand on the throttle to accelerate out of the corner. Do that with a direct-drive kart, and the engine will bog down, since it is not in the ideal engine rpm range, and you will be dog-slow coming out of the corner.

Track Surface Irregularities

One other factor comes into play in finding the ideal line, and that is whether the corner has any elevation changes, banking, bumps, or track surface changes.

The general rule is this: most times, it is better to drive where the track offers more grip or traction than to drive the perfect line.

In other words, if you have to drive over some large bumps or a slippery piece of track to follow the ideal line, you are probably better off driving around the surface changes or irregularities.

Traction is your prime concern. Always drive on the part of the track that offers the most traction. That often means compromising the ideal line for a smoother, grippier path through the corner. The same thing applies to any banking in a corner. If the corner is banked early in the turn and then flattens out, you will probably want to do most of your turning early on and then allow the kart to follow a straighter path on the less-banked part of the track. Again, the goal is to use the surface to your advantage.

Common Errors

Let's face it, everyone makes mistakes, even racers. In fact, one of the things that turns a good racer into a great racer is his ability to minimize—and learn from—his errors. Some drivers make an error, fall off the track, and don't learn a thing from it. Other drivers make an error, alter their technique to keep the kart on the track, and learn that, with a little fine-tuning, this new technique actually results in going faster.

One of the keys to minimizing the effects of an error is learning to identify very early when you have made it, rather than only becoming aware of it a fraction of a second before you have a big crash.

For example, one of the most common errors any driver makes is turning into a corner too early. If you turn into a corner too early, it causes you to apex too early. If you apex too early, one of two things will happen:

- You are going to run out of room at the exit of the turn, probably resulting in your going off the track; or

- You are going to have to turn the steering wheel more sharply to avoid driving off the track. As we already saw, if you tighten up the radius of a turn, you are going to have to slow down. Slowing down in a corner is not a good thing anytime, but it especially hurts at the exit of a corner when you are supposed to be accelerating onto the straightaway.

Obviously, given the choice between the two, you would take the second one, for at least you stay on the track. The only way to do that, though, is to recognize the fact that you've made the error of turning in too early well before reaching the apex of the corner. If you think about it, that should not be too difficult. After all, you know—or at least you should know—precisely where the apex is. If you get to the inside edge of the track before reaching the apex, you probably turned in too early, and you will run out of track at the exit of the corner if you don't make a correction.

In fact, if you are not unwinding (straightening) the steering from at least the apex area on out, you probably turned in too early for the corner. Next time around, try turning in later.

Notice we've said "probably" a few times. That's because there is another error that can cause the same effect of apexing early and running out of track. In this case, the error is turning in too abruptly. In fact, you can sometimes turn in at the exact right point, but because you turn the steering wheel so quickly and sharply, you end up apexing early.

Again, as long as you recognize that you have apexed early, immediately begin making your correction by easing off the throttle (or delaying getting on the throttle), tightening up the radius of the turn, and getting back on the correct line from the apex on out to the exit.

Another fairly common error is trying to carry too much speed into a corner. The result, in this case, is that you spend most of the remainder of the turn attempting to get the kart back under control, and therefore your corner exit speed suffers—a lot. Given the option—and, for the most part, you are—you are better to go into the corners relatively slow and come out fast.

Having said that, another error, though not as common, occurs when a driver over-slows the kart on the entry to the corner. The result is that his cornering speed is relatively slow and he never fully recoups the speed taken off. In other words, he has lost too much momentum and will have a difficult time regaining it.

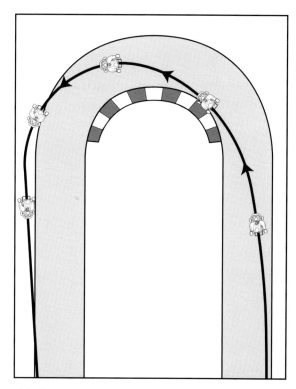

This illustration shows what happens when you turn in too early for a corner: you apex early and run out of track at the exit. It also illustrates why it is so important to have a good turn-in reference point—so you don't turn in too early.

With any error you make—and you will make some—minimize its effect as early as possible, and learn from it. That does not mean dwell on it, or focus on it—there is no point in thinking about a mistake you made in turn two while you are heading into turn three. But do think about it once you've stopped, determining what happened, why you did what you did (were you distracted, did you lose your concentration, were you trying a new technique or approach?), what you can learn from it (maybe this line would work when passing someone), and how you can ensure it doesn't happen again (use a better turn-in reference point, for example).

Making errors isn't a bad thing as long as you use them to learn and improve.

Learning the Track

Learning a track is not a difficult thing to do, as long as you have a plan. Trying to go out and learn everything about a track all at one time is difficult, and maybe even impossible. For most people, their brains are just not capable of taking in too much all at once. So you need a plan, a strategy, for learning a track.

The strategy we recommend is for you to focus on learning any track in the following order:
- The line
- Corner exit
- Corner entry

Your first priority is learning the line around the track, because until driving the ideal line has become a habit, you will have a difficult time increasing your speed. So, keeping in mind that the corners leading onto the straightaways are the most important, the corners at the end of straightaways second most important, and the corners that connect other corners are the least important, work on finding the ideal line. To do that,

Winning drivers walk tracks to learn as much as possible about the line, track surface irregularities, where it is safe to run off the track, and more. Make it part of your regular routine.

start by driving all corners with very late turn-ins and apexes. With each lap, move your turn-in and apex a little earlier and earlier until you feel as though you are running out of track space at the exit of the corner. Then, move it back a bit later again.

Your next priority is maximizing your corner exit speed. That means working toward beginning your acceleration earlier and earlier. Your goal is to get down the straightaway as quickly as possible. Remember, it is always easier to pass your competitors on the straight than in the corners, so do whatever it takes to maximize your straightaway speed.

Finally, work on carrying as much speed as possible into the corners. However, if your increase in corner entry speed begins to hurt your exit speed onto a straightaway, slow down. Exit speed always takes precedence over entry speed on corners leading onto straights.

One thing you should definitely do to help you learn the track is to walk it—no matter how many times you've driven it. There are

things (reference points, track surface irregularities, and so on) that you can only notice at a walking pace. Some drivers only walk a track before the first time they drive it, and then never do it again. We believe it is just as important—maybe more important—to walk the track after you have driven it. The idea is to reinforce what you have seen at speed, but now at a pace where it can really sink in.

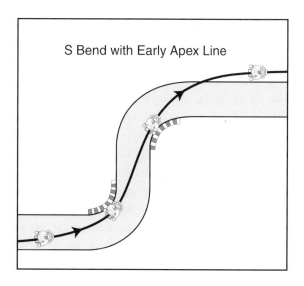

S Bend with Early Apex Line

5
Control Skills

As in any form of motorsport, you first must learn to drive fast, then you can learn to race. With the basics that we covered in the first four chapters in mind, let's dive into what it takes to drive a kart as fast as possible, at the limit.

But first, what do we mean by driving at the limit? We mean having the four tires of the kart at their very limit, or threshold, where even another one-tenth of a mile per hour would put them beyond and cause the kart to slide too much—possibly even spin out.

After you get so that you can drive the kart on the ideal line on a consistent basis, the key to being fast is driving the kart at the limit in each phase of the corners: the entry, the middle, and the exit. In reality, the order of these objectives should change. Your first priority, after getting the cornering line down pat, is to perfect the exit or acceleration phase. After that, you should work on the corner entry phase, carrying more and more speed into the corner to the point just before it negatively affects your acceleration out of the

corner. And then, finally, you should work on smoothly carrying more speed through the middle of the corners.

Momentum Revisited

As we mentioned in the last chapter, an overall, general rule that must be kept in mind at all times when driving any type of kart is this: Momentum is everything. Momentum is critical.

Momentum is even more critical with a direct-drive kart, since there is no clutch (as in a clutch kart) or gears (as in a shifter kart). If you over-slow a direct-drive kart by even one mile per hour, the engine does not have the benefit of a clutch or gears to help keep the engine in the ideal rev range. Instead, the engine will bog down (the engine's rpm dropping below the ideal range, to a point where it has a difficult time gaining speed again).

In a clutch or shifter kart the rule is to keep the revs up. That's not too difficult with a shifter kart—you simply select a lower gear by downshifting. With a clutch kart, though, it's not as simple.

Driving a kart's limit through turns is a challenge. The more knowledge and the better your understanding of what the limit is, the better you can deal with the challenge.

The ideal engine rev range—the rpm range where the engine produces its maximum power and pulls or accelerates the strongest—is near the top of the overall range. It is usually in the last three or four thousand rpm before the engine's redline. If the engine revs drop too low below this ideal range, you will spend a lot of time building them back up again, and it will slow down your acceleration.

Therefore, you must drive in such a way as to keep the revs up. While driving through a corner with a clutch kart this often means anticipating when the clutch is going to engage and getting on the throttle earlier than needed while the centrifugal clutch is partially disengaged. If the clutch is set up properly, it will allow the engine to rev without it trying to drive the kart forward, until you squeeze down fully on the throttle.

While doing this, of course, you are trying to drive a line that enables you to slow the kart as little as possible. Remember, every time you slow a kart down, you are going to have to accelerate it back up to speed again. And that takes time—time wasted if you could have driven the corner without slowing it as much.

So momentum is all-important, because you don't want the engine to bog down. But there is another reason as well. As you probably know, karts do not have a differential like cars

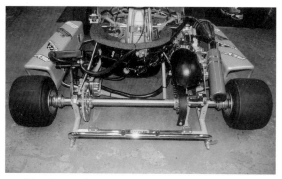

As this photo demonstrates, all karts have a solid rear axle, which is the main difference between karts and cars. It is also the main reason karts need to be setup and driven the way they do. The only way to get a kart to turn—change direction—is to unload the inside rear tire, to have it practically lift off the track surface.

(hence, the name differential) speeds—the inside traveling slower than the outside.

Since a kart has a solid rear axle with no ability to compensate for this difference in distance traveled by the inside and outside rear wheels, the inside tire scrubs. Think about it. As the kart is going around every corner, while the outside tire is rolling along the track surface, the inside tire is being forced to turn faster than necessary to cover the distance, or the opposite happens—the inside tire rolls along the surface and the outside tire slips. In reality, a bit of both happens, but the result is the tires scrubbing against the track surface.

So, every time you turn the steering wheel on a kart, the rear tires begin to scrub. The result is almost like applying the brakes.

To get a good feeling for how important this is, try this demonstration with a kart sitting on a flat paved or concrete surface. Holding the steering wheel with one hand, and the back of the seat with the other, push your kart

do. They have a solid rear axle. When any four-wheeled vehicle goes around a corner, the wheels on the inside of the turn have less distance to travel, as they are following a tighter radius. What a car's differential does is allow the inside and outside wheels to travel at different

Shown here is a rear tire in the heat of the action in a turn: acting like a spring (absorbing the bumps), handling the cornering loads, gripping the track, and sliding all at one time. When you see a photo such as this, it makes you realize just how much tires do for you.

in a straight line. Notice how much effort it takes. Now, turn the steering wheel in one direction or the other and push it. How much effort does it take then? Much more, right? This is what the engine has to overcome every time you turn the steering wheel.

All things being equal, the driver who turns the steering wheel the least will be the fastest. Remember, turning the steering wheel is a terrible, terrible thing to do to a kart! So, keep the front wheels pointing as straight as possible, as much as possible. Let the kart run free.

Castor Effect

Let's take a look at something called the castor effect. Way back when, someone discovered that if he changed the angle of the spindle (the part of the chassis that the front wheels attach to that allows them to steer) on his cart (that is, horse-drawn cart, not go-kart), it would more easily track in a straight line. In fact, he could practically let go of the steering controls and it would continue to steer straight. Even after turning the steering mechanism, it would have the tendency to straighten out on its own.

When the automobile replaced the horse and cart, this idea was adapted, as it was when the first kart was built. If you turn the steering wheel on your kart, and then push it, it will straighten out by itself. Again, that is due to the angle of the spindle—the castor angle.

This castor effect has one other great, unique benefit on a kart—one that is not a factor with cars. To see this, place a kart on a flat surface with its front tires pointing straight ahead. Then, turn the steering wheel and notice what happens to the chassis. The angle of the spindle, the castor, causes the inside front tire to be driven downward, lifting the inner side of the chassis; while the outside tire moves upward in

Here the front tires/wheels are pointing straight ahead, and the chassis is level with the ground.

This photo shows the effect of castor. When the front tires are turned to the left, the left-side tire is driven downward, lifting that corner of the chassis, while the right front tire rises, lowering that side of the chassis. This unloading of the chassis on the inside of a corner is what takes weight off of the inside rear tire and allows the kart to turn.

relation to the chassis, allowing the outside of the chassis to drop.

The main benefit of this effect is that it takes weight off the inside rear tire as the steering wheel is turned. Why is that important? Remember what we said about how the inside rear tire follows a tighter, or smaller, radius through a corner, and that it scrubs through the corner. Because the rear axle is solid, it has a tendency to drive the kart straight ahead.

Every time you apply the gas or brake pedal, think about squeezing them as if they were sponges.

The castor, however, by lifting weight off of the inside rear tire, allows it to scrub less. In fact, without the castor, it would be very difficult to make a kart change direction.

Three Things You Can Do with a Kart

As we said earlier, there are only three things you can do with a kart. You can steer, you can accelerate, and you can brake.

The key to going fast in a kart is to do these three things as smoothly as possible. Yes, you must be somewhat aggressive to get the very last ounce of speed out of the kart, but you must do that with as much smoothness and finesse as you can. In fact, most people are very surprised when they finally learn just how much finesse this sport really requires. Many people think that race driving any type of kart or car is all about recklessly and aggressively careening around the track. They are wrong! In fact, the smoother you drive, the faster you will be. Actually, the less you do of two of those three things—steer and brake—the faster you will be. You will have more grip and less scrubbing the less you turn the steering wheel. And if you get on and off the brakes less you will have more grip, not to mention more momentum. It almost goes without saying that the more grip you have, the faster you can drive.

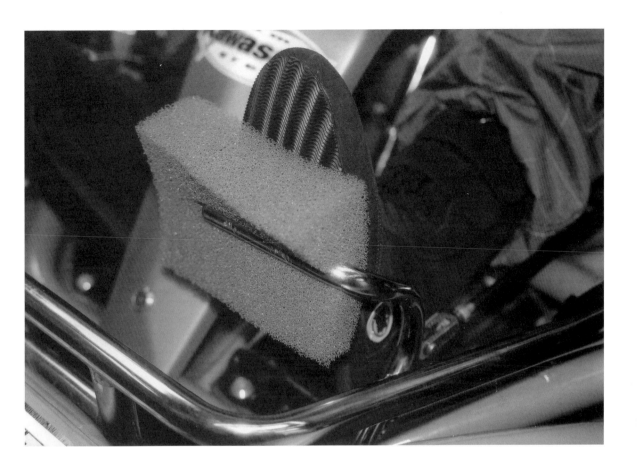

Using the Pedals

How, exactly, do you use the gas pedal and the brake pedal? Smooth, smooth, smooth, and with feel. Think of the gas and brake pedals as two sponges. You squeeze the pedals down, right foot on the throttle and left foot on the brakes, as though you are squeezing water out of them.

After accelerating down a straightaway with your foot to the floor on the gas, don't lift off the throttle too abruptly. Roll off it quickly, but smoothly. This way, you control the weight transfer. If you have to brake for the corner, then as you roll off the gas, squeeze on the brakes at the same time with your left foot.

Human nature dictates that if you lift off the throttle fast at the end of a straightaway, you are going to brake hard—probably too hard. But if you roll off smoother, you'll squeeze the brakes on. Squeeze the brakes on and you will slow down quicker than if you slammed on the brakes.

Squeezing on the brakes does not mean braking slowly or softly. It just means be very smooth with the way you apply it so that you will maintain the most traction possible.

You may be thinking, "I thought racing was all about going fast? How do you squeeze and ease the pedals fast? How do you roll off the gas fast?" It's a matter of practice, thinking of

Braking is used for much more than just slowing the kart. It is also a means of changing balance and direction. Having a sensitive feel for the brake pedal is one of the keys to being fast.

squeezing and easing the pedals, and sensing and feeling the balance of the kart. If you are aware of the balance of the kart, you will naturally be smoother with the controls. It's one of the biggest challenges in driving a kart—the balance between doing everything as quickly as possible while doing it as smoothly as possible.

Braking with a kart is far more tricky than one would initially think, for several reasons.

A kart's lack of suspension means that there may be times when you are barely in contact with the track. Controlling the kart at that instant is very tricky; using the brakes and throttle smoothly while you and the kart are bouncing all around is a real challenge. That is one of the reasons the fit of your seat is so important—to hold your body in place.

First, because most people do not use their left foot for braking when driving their vehicle on the street, they have never developed the sensitivity required. And if you happen to drive a vehicle with a standard transmission, your left foot is in the habit of only depressing the clutch pedal with each shift. The first time you go to use it for braking, you may find yourself stabbing at the kart's brake pedal very abruptly. If you haven't reached the age yet where you are driving a car on the street, this is an advantage for you—you don't have a habit that needs to be broken.

The second reason braking is so challenging in a kart is simply due to the lack of suspension. Karts tend to bounce and vibrate all over the track. That makes it very difficult to control your foot to allow the necessary modulation of the brakes. Many times, just when you go to apply the brakes, you hit some bumps and your left foot practically bounces out of the kart. That makes it a bit tricky to squeeze the brakes with sensitivity. Brake too lightly and you may not slow the kart enough for the corner; brake too hard and you will lock up the brakes and find yourself spinning down the track.

The last reason braking is difficult is that karts stop so quickly—faster than you can imagine. Until you have spent time in a serious racing kart, it is difficult to fathom just how quickly they can stop.

A lot of drivers, especially when they first start driving karts, use the brake pedal like an on-off switch. It is not meant to be used—actually, abused—like this. The problem is that such drivers do not have the habit of squeezing the pedal with their left foot. The cure, obviously, is practice—practice squeezing the brake pedal down with as much smoothness as possible, and then easing off of it. Remember: squeeze and ease the pedals!

The balance and overlapping of braking and throttle should be like a dance—smooth, flowing, precise, and natural. Your transition from on the gas to on the brakes, and vice versa, should be seamless; you should not be able to feel the exact point where one ends and the other begins.

Many drivers also have a tendency to suddenly lift off the brake pedal as they turn into the corner, and then coast for a while before squeezing back on the gas. Karts do not like to be coasted. They feel as though they are at the very edge—or beyond—when you are coasting, even when you are a long way below the "at the limit" speed. Being on the throttle will actually make the kart grip the track even better.

So the rule is always be on either the brake or the throttle. If you are not either applying the brakes or the throttle, you are coasting. There is no place in racing for coasting. Since

you have two feet and two pedals to operate you can actually intermingle or overlap the two slightly—for a fraction of a second.

Notice we said for a fraction of a second—a slight overlap of the braking and accelerating. This does not mean doing what is called "power braking"—applying the brakes to slow down while keeping your foot on the throttle at the same time. Although this can feel fast, it rarely is. And if you are using this technique when driving a clutch kart, you will most likely require a new clutch by the end of the day; if you are driving a

For most karts, this is all that stops them: one brake on the rear axle (125-cc shifter karts have brakes on both front wheels). Yet on a vehicle as light as a kart, that's a lot of braking power—enough to get you in trouble if you brake too hard and lock up the rear tires.

direct-drive kart, it will cause so much heat to build up in the engine that it will either lose power or break.

Most karts have brakes only on the rear axle. If you think about what braking might do to the kart while going around a corner with the brakes applied on the rear axle, it suggests that you should do *most* of your braking in a straight line approaching the corner. If you are braking too much as you turn the steering wheel to enter a corner, it may cause the kart to oversteer.

Go back to our earlier discussion about how you can only use 100 percent of the tires' traction, and not any more. If you are braking at even 50 percent when you turn into the corner, there is a good chance that the rear tires will exceed their 100 percent (because you are asking for more than 50 percent of their traction for cornering) and begin to give up their grip and slide sideways—oversteer.

That is why you want to do most of the braking in the straight line approaching a corner. But keep in mind how fast a kart can slow down. The straight line where you are braking before the corner may be as short as a foot or two.

With that in mind, though, one of the keys to going really fast in a kart is learning to brake into the corner—sometimes as far as to the apex. This is called *trail braking*. What we are talking about is doing most of your braking—at the tires' traction limit—on the straight approaching the turn, then gradually easing—trailing–off the brakes as you turn into the corner. Depending on the corner and the kart, that trail braking may last for a foot into the corner, or all the way to the apex. One of the objectives is to keep the tires at their traction limit throughout the braking and cornering areas of the track.

This photo clearly shows the inside rear tire lifting off the track surface just slightly. Caused by the castor, the chassis flex, and the weight transfer to the outside in a corner, this is what provides the "differential" and allows the kart to turn.

By the way, trail braking is a technique that, once learned, will bode well for the future. It is the preferred technique for driving really fast in practically any type of race car.

Can you think of another reason for using trail braking in a kart?

Remember what we learned about weight transfer in chapter 2, and that a kart has a solid rear axle, causing it to want to continue driving in a straight line when you want it to turn. The only way you can make a kart turn is to unload the inside rear tire. If you can make that tire lift off the track surface, the kart will easily turn wherever you want it to. Entering the turn with the brakes applied loads the outside front tire and lifts the inside rear. This allows the kart to rotate or change direction. But the second you touch the throttle, the inside rear sits back down on the track and the kart will shift toward understeer.

So as you approach a turn, roll off the throttle and brake at the very limit of traction on the straightaway, using up 100 percent of the tires' traction for slowing the kart down. Then, as you begin to turn into the corner, ease, or trail, your foot off the brake pedal. Somewhere between the turn-in point and the apex area—once the kart is rotated around the corner enough, and while you are still trailing off the brakes—start squeezing on the throttle. Now you have a slight overlap of the braking and throttle, with the goal of being off the brakes and back to full throttle by the time you reach the apex. The exact point to make this transition from braking to acceleration depends on the radius, length, any elevation change, and banking of the corner, along with the amount of traction you have and the handling characteristics of your kart.

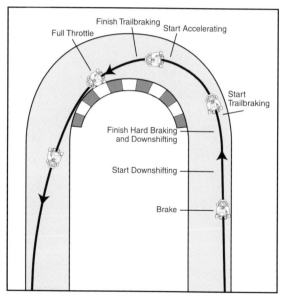

This illustration indicates the different phases you go through as you drive through a turn. Obviously, the reference to downshifting applies to shifter karts, although everything else applies equally to any type of kart.

In the illustration labels: Finish Trailbraking, Full Throttle, Start Accelerating, Start Trailbraking, Finish Hard Braking and Downshifting, Start Downshifting, Brake

This may call for a bit of patience. It is tempting sometimes to immediately get back on the throttle once you've turned into the corner. But if you don't have the kart rotated around the turn enough, beginning to accelerate too early may mean you are just going to have to lift off the throttle again later in the corner. That is going to kill your momentum as you accelerate onto the straightaway.

However, never forget that the driver who gets on the gas the soonest will usually get down the straightaway the fastest.

If you begin accelerating too early or too hard at this point, you may also cause the kart to oversteer. If you have too much steering angle dialed in when the inside rear tire sits down, along with a lot of acceleration, the rear tires may also lose grip and want to come around. Again, although your goal is to begin

accelerating as early as possible, it sometimes takes a little patience as well.

This type of oversteer, caused by getting on the throttle too hard, is called *power-oversteer*. Primarily this is only going to happen in the higher-powered karts, and it occurs when you accelerate so hard that you cause some wheel spin, which kicks out the rear end of the kart. This usually feels great, and looks great, but only rarely is it the fast way to drive. Typically, it is only effective when trying to get the kart to rotate around a fairly tight turn. In most other situations, the wheel spin only reduces the kart's cornering and acceleration abilities.

Throttle control, especially in a shifter kart, is one of the keys to being fast. You must be as smooth and delicate as possible as you roll on the throttle. If not, the resulting wheel spin or unbalancing of the kart will mean not accelerating as quickly as possible. Your goal should be to squeeze on the throttle as early as possible in the corner, rolling it on to full throttle, instead of using it like an on-off switch. Always remember, the sooner you get back to full throttle without causing any wheel spin, the faster you will be down the straightaway.

The more time you spend with your right foot down hard on the throttle, the quicker you will be. That doesn't mean you should use the throttle like an on-off switch. Instead, squeeze it on, even if that means squeezing it on very quickly.

Again, the key is to progressively squeeze down on the throttle, at a rate that does not overload the rear tires. Even in a non-shifter kart, where smashing down on the throttle probably won't induce wheel spin, you still want to roll onto the throttle. If you get on the throttle too quickly, too aggressively, you will probably make the kart understeer by unweighting the front tires. If that happens, you are going to have to ease up on the throttle slightly to avoid running off the edge of the track at the corner exit. Easing off the throttle is going to kill your momentum.

The driver in this photo has entered a corner while trail braking heavily, which has caused the kart to oversteer dramatically. In this case, he has asked the rear tires for more than 100 percent, and they began to slide sideways in response.

Back to our 100 percent traction rule. There are times when you may deliberately want to push past 100 percent just ever so slightly with the rear tires (of course, pushing past 100 percent, like dropping below it, results in a decrease of traction). You would do this when using the brakes to help steer the kart. In this case, as you enter the turn you trail brake, only this time you use slightly more than 100 percent of the rear tires' traction.

For example, let's say you are already using up 100 percent of the tires' traction in a combination of trail braking and cornering, but you want the kart to rotate or turn a little more before reaching the apex. If you turned the steering wheel more, the front tires would just slide more (remember, you are already using 100 percent of their traction). But in a kart with rear brakes only, if you squeeze on just a little more brake, the rear tires will exceed 100 percent traction, causing the rear of the kart to slide sideways toward

the outside of the turn (oversteer). Of course, you must then quickly get back on the throttle once the kart has rotated enough, otherwise you will oversteer yourself right into a spin.

Understand, we are talking about only adding 1 or 2 percent more braking to get the rear of the kart to slide. If you brake more than that, the kart will most likely go into a very quick spin. You can see from this example why it is so important to have a very sensitive feel for the brakes, and the ability to precisely modulate them.

Steering

As we said earlier, you want to turn the steering wheel as little as possible, being as smooth and precise as possible. If you execute the corner properly, you will turn the steering wheel only once at the turn-in point, and then unwind it at the right time to end up at the ideal exit point of the corner. If you turn the wheel more than that, you are scrubbing off speed. You do not want to "saw" at the wheel. Steering any more than necessary slows you down.

Never forget that the less you turn the steering wheel, the faster you will go, since you will have scrubbed off less speed with the front tires. It's rare that you will ever have to turn the steering wheel much more than this to get around any turn on a track.

The key to being smooth with your steering input is looking well ahead. We'll talk about this in more detail in chapter 7.

As we said earlier, your hands should sit comfortably at around the 2 and 10 o'clock positions on the steering wheel, with a slight bend in the elbows. When you turn the wheel, your hand on the outside of the turn should do most of the work, pushing up on the wheel. By pushing up and forward on the steering wheel, you are actually transferring more weight onto the outside front tire.

That is not to say the inside hand does nothing. It is dampening any non-smooth movements, making the steering inputs more precise.

There is a "trick" that some really good kart drivers use to make the weight transfer produce a further benefit. As they turn into a corner,

they lock their outside arm at the elbow, while holding the steering wheel. The forces from the front tires are then transmitted back through the steering column, through the driver's hand, up his arm, through the shoulder to the seat, down the seat supports, and onto the outside rear tire. If the driver's arm is flexing, this force will not go past his elbow. This trick can also be used to help the handling of the kart. If the kart is oversteering, lock your outside arm; if it's understeering, let it flex.

Is this a technique that you need to learn when you first start racing karts? No, it's a somewhat advanced technique. However, if you start practicing it now it will help you to excel more quickly and advance to a higher level.

Shifter Kart Shifting

Shifter karts have really become popular in the past few years for a variety of reasons,

The driver in this photo has locked his left arm (keeping his arm completely straight and locked at the elbow) while driving through this right-hander. He does this to help put more load on the left front tire, to increase its grip. So by locking or unlocking your arm, you can change the kart's handling significantly.

With a six-speed gearbox and acceleration similar to a Champ car, everything happens quickly; you are very busy in a shifter kart! This driver is shifting while exiting a corner.

such as their outright speed, their reliability, and the extra challenge of having to shift. This last point, having to shift, is something new to many kart racers who have only driven direct-drive and clutch karts. Shifting a shifter kart is just different enough from cars that people who have never driven one find it a bit difficult at first.

Getting behind the wheel and driving a shifter kart for the first time is a real eye-opener. The quickness, the acceleration, the braking, and the cornering are second only to a Formula One or CART Champ car. The biggest mistakes a driver new to shifters makes are not using the engine right and shifting poorly—usually resulting in the kart driving the driver,

rather than the driver driving the kart. The key is being relaxed, not over-revving the engine, and making good, clean, precise shifts. How fast you shift is not nearly as important as when you shift and how accurately you shift. Most of the time, shifting at a slightly lower rpm is better than too high. An engine at very high rpm is overly sensitive to throttle movements, making the kart very difficult to drive—especially over bumpy sections of track.

Shifter kart engines and transmissions are either directly out of motocross bikes or are derived from them. Therefore, the shifting action is identical to shifting a motorcycle.

The first thing to get used to is the fact that you do not use the clutch to shift. Once the

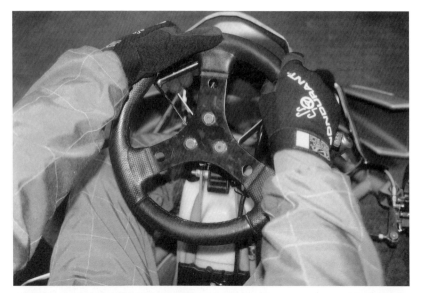

The clutch control on a shifter kart is a paddle-type handle attached to the steering column, and is operated with the left hand. Once you initially get the kart moving, you never use it again until you come to a stop.

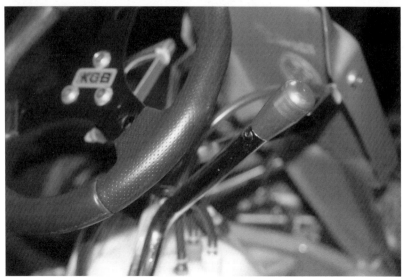

The shift lever on a shifter kart is mounted right next to the steering wheel, so that when shifting your right hand is off the steering wheel for the least amount of time possible. Your right hand should hold the steering wheel, come off quickly to shift, and then get back on the wheel immediately.

engine is running, the only times you use the clutch are to get moving and when you come to a stop. For every other shift you make, all the way from first to top gear (usually sixth) and back again, you simply pull the shift lever back toward you to shift up, or push it away from you to downshift. As you pull or push the lever to upshift or downshift, you must lift your foot off of the throttle, just as you would when shifting a car. But don't touch the clutch.

The second thing to get used to is the fact that the clutch is not a pedal, but a paddle-type lever that you pull up on with your left hand to disengage. When you consider that you need to use your left hand for the clutch (to get started and stopped), your right hand to shift up and down the six gears, and both to steer, you understand why shifters are such a challenging thrill.

The shift pattern is not the typical H-pattern that you would find in a car. The

Shown here is a shifter kart driver at speed, in the middle of shifting gears.

shifter only moves backward and forward in a straight line. To get it into first gear, you click the shift lever forward, then release it, click it forward, then release it, and so on until it doesn't click forward anymore. That's first gear. Neutral is between first and second gears, so to engage neutral you would pull back just slightly—if you pull back too far it will shift into second.

To engage second gear, you pull all the way back, as you would to engage third, fourth, fifth, and sixth, making sure you release the shifter after each shift. If you ride a motorcycle, you'll recognize this pattern.

Downshifting is the exact opposite. You just click it forward and release the lever for each downshift. And if you have learned to

heel and toe, or blip the throttle to match the engine revs with a car, forget it. There is no need to match the revs—just click it into the next-lower gear. Again, it is important to ensure that you release the shift lever after each shift. If you hold pressure against the lever, you will never be able to make the next shift. Besides, you definitely need both hands on the steering wheel to control these little rockets!

There are two alternatives for starting a shifter kart engine. In the first, you sit in the kart with the gearbox in neutral and have someone push the kart (pushing on the back of the seat). You know from the demonstration of the solid rear axle that this should be done in a straight line, rather than while turning. Once

Demonstrated here is the hand position for upshifting a shifter kart. You simply pull back on the lever to shift up a gear.

This is the hand position for downshifting, just pushing forward on the shift lever.

the kart is moving, you simply click the shifter forward—putting it in first gear—and give it a bit of throttle to get the engine running. This is just like jump-starting a car, only you don't need to use the clutch.

A word of warning here for the person pushing: once the engine begins to start, let go of the kart. It may take off very quickly and if you're still holding it you can easily fall on your face.

You can use the second method of starting a shifter kart when you have a little experience. Start with the kart pointing down a straight section of track and you on the left side of it. Grab the top of the steering wheel with your left hand, and the top of the back of the seat

Shown here is a shifter kart driver getting a push start. It's imperative for the person who is pushing to let go of the kart just prior to the engine firing up.

with your right hand. Start pushing it, running alongside. Once you get it rolling as fast as you can, while still holding the steering wheel, jump onto the seat with your right foot, bring the left foot over, and plop yourself into the seat as quickly as possible. As you are doing this, get your right foot on the throttle as fast as you can, knock the shifter forward into first gear and give it some gas. With any luck at all, the engine will fire up and you will accelerate away. With any bad luck (actually, bad timing or not enough speed), you will trip and fall on your face or the kart engine will not start. Either way, you will have to try it all over again (which is one of the reasons for all your physical training!). Actually, this sounds more difficult than it really is.

If you are about to drive a shifter kart for the very first time, you should probably do what we do at the Bondurant SuperKart School for first-timers. Find a straight piece of track or a large parking lot, and set a pylon near each end. Get the kart started, accelerate up through all six gears toward one pylon, downshift back through the gears to first, turn around the pylon and accelerate back up through the gears and back down again, and around the second pylon.

Keep on doing this until you are fully comfortable with the shifting technique. There is no point in trying to drive around a track, worrying about the corners, while you are learning how to shift. You will just waste time and energy, and probably get frustrated.

To push-start a shifter kart by yourself, start by pushing the kart like this, and then hop into the seat and knock the shifter into gear. The key is to push the kart fast enough that it has the momentum to give you sufficient time to get halfway into the kart and into gear.

Using Your Body Weight

Karts do not have seat belts to hold the driver in place. The extra movement that this allows you can be used to your advantage—especially since your weight represents a significant portion of the total weight of vehicle and driver. Typically, the weight of a driver is anything from 30 to 50 percent of the overall driver/kart combination. By shifting this weight around, you can alter the weight distribution of the kart and improve traction.

The main idea of shifting your weight is to move your upper body, leaning it to the outside of the turn, causing more weight to transfer onto the outside rear tire. Notice we said leaning to the outside of the turn. For many people, this seems unnatural—they feel as though they should lean into the corner. In fact, leaning into the corner does nothing at best, and hurts your kart's handling at worst.

This technique does take considerable practice to get the timing and amount of movement just right. But when you do, it can increase the kart's cornering grip significantly. It is used most often on wet surfaces, but can be used on dry surfaces as well. In dry conditions, the movements may be a bit more sub-

Here's a driver at the Bondurant SuperKart School practicing his shifting technique. Students accelerate up through the gears, downshift back down, turn around a cone, and do it all over again.

tle. In the rain, the movements may be more exaggerated, as it may be the only way to get the kart to rotate in a corner.

Typically, this technique would be used in two different situations. The first is when going through a reasonably fast corner. In this case, your body movement—leaning your upper body toward the outside of the turn—should be done slowly and gently. If you are not gentle enough with this, it could overload the outside rear tire and upset the balance of the kart. The ideal is to ease your weight over to the outside, which puts more weight on the outside tires, especially the rear tire. If the kart

immediately starts sliding when you do this, you have done it too much.

The second situation is when driving through a tight corner, or any time you need the kart to change directions quickly or rotate better. In this case, your body movement should be a little more violent—throw your body weight forward and to the side.

For example, if you are approaching a hairpin turn in the wet, the first problem you face is just getting the kart to turn. It wants to plow straight ahead. The only way to get the kart to turn is to load the front tires and unload the inside rear. The effect of the castor

A driver can alter the kart's handling and grip level by shifting his own body weight. In this photo, the driver is leaning his body to the outside to load the outside tires, thereby increasing their traction. This is a technique you should experiment with and practice. It may come in handy in overcoming a handling problem.

we talked about earlier will help initiate this transfer. But sometimes all the castor in the world won't allow the kart to change direction quickly enough for your circumstances. In that case, throwing your body weight forward and to the outside loads the front tires and lifts the inside tire even more.

Although this can be a useful technique, often you'll be better off just concentrating on being smooth. Throwing your weight around can easily upset the balance of the kart, so if you do it, do it with smoothness and finesse. That will take practice and experience.

Karting in the Rain

It really is amazing how often karters pack up and go home as soon as it starts raining. If they only knew just how valuable practicing on a wet track can be—if they realized just how great a learning opportunity it is—they would instead be *looking* for rainy days. It not only helps you become better in the wet, it helps equally in making you better in the dry. Wet-track driving helps you develop a better feel for where the traction limit is, and it demands super-smoothness, which is always worth practicing.

Racing karts in the rain is an extra challenge that great drivers truly enjoy, although the biggest challenge is often just being able to see through the spray. It is very important to apply an antifog agent to the inside of your helmet visor. *GO Racing Magazine*

So even though you and your kart will get wet, and it can take a bit of work to change the chassis setup to suit the rain, practice in the wet every chance you get. If you are not into making changes to the chassis, don't. Just bolt on some rain tires and get out there.

We have stressed how important being smooth is in the dry. Well, multiply that by 10 for the rain. If you are a little too aggressive with the brakes, you will spin. If you are too aggressive with the steering wheel, you will spin. If you are too aggressive with the throttle, you will spin. Do you see the pattern

here? Learning to drive fast in the rain is an exercise in smoothness.

As a general rule, you should change the line you drive on a wet track. Your main goal for doing this is to find a line that gives the tires more grip. On most tracks, the dry line has been polished smooth by all the karts sliding over it. It is also where the most rubber and oil are laid down on the pavement. When this gets wet, it will offer the least amount of grip. So drive elsewhere. Usually, that means driving around the outside of the turn—or at least around the outside of the dry line.

The driver of this kart got on the throttle too hard while exiting a corner with too much steering input, and spun the kart around. If he had unwound (straightened) the steering wheel sooner, he probably would not have spun.

Of course, every track and every turn is different, so you need to search constantly for the grippiest pavement—and this can change from lap to lap.

An advanced technique that can be used to get the kart to change direction and turn quicker in the wet is to quickly crank the steering wheel to full lock when you first turn into the corner, and then unwind it from there. This approach takes full advantage of the kart's castor effect, loading the front tires as much as possible and getting the inside rear tire to lift fully off the ground. At the same time, by doing this you can use the scrubbing of the front tires to help slow the kart down.

When you turn the wheel to full lock, do it very quickly. Since all the weight is on the front tires and relatively little on the rears, once the kart begins to turn it is easy to spin. For this reason, as soon as it turns, quickly unwind the steering.

Yes, this goes against what we said about turning the steering wheel as little as possible to maintain momentum, but you do it for such a short period of time that the benefit of helping get the kart turned outweighs the negative effect of scrubbing off some speed. Further, using this technique intentionally to scrub off some speed may be useful, although the amount of scrub on a wet track is minimal.

This is not a technique to be used in all types of karts. You must experiment with your kart to determine if it is appropriate.

Spins

Many spins in a kart come early in a turn when you have some amount of braking still applied—while you are trail braking. With this in mind, it should be relatively easy to correct the problem before you completely spin. The very second you feel the rear of the kart begin to slide, just ease up on the brakes slightly. The reason the kart starts to spin is that you are asking for more than 100 percent from the rear tires.

Of course, some spins come from attempting to carry too much speed into a corner. The biggest problem with entering a turn too quickly is not necessarily the speed; it is your reaction to the speed. Most people, once they realize they have made the error of going too fast, either freeze up and don't do much of anything to correct for it, or they overreact. Both responses typically lead to a spin.

Be aware that most spins do not cause any harm to either you or your kart. And if you know what caused the spin, you can often learn something that leads to an improvement in your driving. If you are going to race karts competitively, and therefore drive the kart at the limit, you will spin every now and then. Great kart drivers learn from their errors; the rest do not.

6
Racecraft

Racecraft is all about passing, being passed, and running in traffic in such a way that you gain an advantage over your competition, or at least minimize the disadvantage. It is also the strategies you use throughout practice, qualifying, and the race to maximize your performance. Great, winning drivers have learned great racecraft skills. The drivers who don't learn will never win or be great.

As we said at the beginning of the last chapter, first you must learn to drive as fast as possible, then you can learn to race. We hope we have given you the information you require to drive consistently at the limit, as fast as you can go. Now it is time to learn racecraft.

Practice

In addition to the obvious objective of having fun driving a kart, the key objectives for any practice session are:
- To learn how to drive faster;
- To learn how to race better; or
- To see what effect certain changes have made to the performance of your kart.

Learning how to drive faster is a constant challenge, no matter how fast you are. Your goal should always be to improve, for it is very difficult to drive a perfect corner, let alone a perfect lap. You can always learn something new that can make you faster.

To do that, you must first be able to drive reasonably consistently, with your lap times not varying any more than a few tenths of a second at most. If your lap times vary more than that, and you make a change to your driving, how are you going to know if it helped?

Once your driving is reasonably consistent, then it is time to begin trying something new: a different line through a corner, braking earlier or later, turning the steering wheel quicker or slower, and so forth. The key then is to be aware of the effect the change had. This can be done simply by making a note of your lap time, or it may be a matter of feel. A good driver does not always need a stopwatch to tell him whether a change was for the better or worse.

Practice is also a good time to watch what other drivers are doing—within reason. Often, when you are following another kart, you can

The wheel-to-wheel competition and racecraft experience gained in one kart race takes many car racers years to learn. Here's an example why—karts everywhere! *GO Racing Magazine*

see things that you or someone else would never have noticed from the side of the track. A word of warning, though, about paying too much attention to your competitors: sometimes you can be fooled into thinking that since another driver can take a corner at a certain speed, that you should be able to as well. Keep in mind that your kart may be set up differently. And you can get so focused on what the others are doing that you are not paying enough attention to what you are doing. Often, if you would only put that much focus on your own performance, you would be miles ahead of the competition, and they would be putting all their attention into what you are doing.

The second point, learning how to race better, is often forgotten or never thought of by most racers. Practice is the time to try out different lines to see how they can help you pass another kart or defend your position, or whether you can gain an advantage by altering it.

Most important, though, you should drive the practice session with the same intensity level you maintain while racing. If you drive a practice session with a casual "this is good enough for practice" attitude, guess what you will be good at doing in the race? Driving with a "good enough" attitude. Whatever you practice you become good at,

Shown here is a typical pack of karts, all fighting for the lead. This is what racecraft is all about: passing, being passed, and re-passing. The wheel-to-wheel dicing may just be the most enjoyable part of kart racing. *GO Racing Magazine*

so practice great driving, not so-so driving. Many drivers spend more time practicing making mistakes, developing bad habits, and doing the wrong things rather than doing the right things. Therefore, they get good at bad things.

Practice does not make perfect. Only perfect practice makes perfect.

If you find yourself getting sloppy in your driving, usually because of either physical or mental fatigue, stop. There is no point practicing the wrong things. This is also why having someone with a trained eye watching you is so important. Before you spend so much time

practicing a mistake that it becomes a habit, an experienced observer can suggest a change, or at least signal you to stop. We're not saying you should never, or will never, make a mistake— only that you want to learn from your mistakes and not repeat them to the point where they come to define your driving. Many times you can learn something from an error that enables you to go even faster. For example, by making the "error" of entering a corner with too much speed, you may find that you can actually make it work. The result is a big reduction in lap time.

The only way you are going to learn anything from your mistakes, though, is to be

A race really begins in qualifying. If you qualify near the back of the pack, it's going to be a real fight to get to the front. This is obviously why qualifying is so important. *GO Racing Magazine*

aware of them, but not critical of them. By that we mean take notice of what happened, then ask yourself what was the real cause of it, and what you can do differently next time to make it work. Making an error, and then thinking to yourself, "you dummy, that was a stupid thing to do," will not help in any way. It will only hurt the situation.

Practice is the time to experiment with some chassis and engine adjustments in the attempt to improve your kart's performance. Again, it is important to be aware of what effect the changes have. And there is no point in making more than one change at a time, for

if you make a multitude of changes and the kart improves, you will have no idea why. One change may have caused the improvement, while others actually hurt the performance.

It is also critical that you make a note of each and every change you make, and the results of each. That is the only way to avoid making the same mistake twice. It is best to draw a map of the track and write down notes about the line you are driving, and how the kart is handling in each turn (and segment of turn). Using a printed map supplied by the track itself is not as meaningful as one drawn by you, since the track will always appear a little different from what an engineering drawing can depict.

Qualifying

Qualifying for any type of racing is important, but it is critical in kart racing. The competition in the races is just too tight to give up a position at the start because you don't qualify well. In other words, if you want to be successful in karting, you will need to learn how to turn in one blisteringly fast lap to qualify as far up the grid as possible.

In some road-racing events, qualifying involves all karts in the class going onto the track at the same time, and whoever turns the quickest lap time in the session is gridded at the front for the race. Other times, though, you will only have two laps in which to achieve your fastest qualifying lap. In that situation, you will be the only kart on the track, and from the time you pull out of the pits you have to go absolutely as fast as possible. In oval-track racing, the procedure is much the same, with one kart on the track at a time for one or two laps. Sometimes the grid will be inverted, with the slowest qualifier in the pole position and fastest at the back of the grid.

The bigger the field, the more important your starting position, as passing can be difficult—and getting by other karts can take up more laps than you have to race. That is why qualifying is so critical. For some drivers, putting in a fast qualifier in just two laps is very difficult—they need a few more laps to get warmed up and in a rhythm. Often, you do not have that luxury, so you will need to learn how to put in an immediate qualifying lap. That means honing this skill during practice sessions.

Many times you will head out for qualifying on new tires. Often, getting that extra couple of tenths or hundredths of a second from new tires is what makes the difference between being at the front of the grid or not. You might be as quick as someone in practice, or just a tenth or so back, but when it comes to qualifying, he's six- or seven-tenths quicker. The difference most likely is that the other driver knows where the limit is for new tires—and makes use of every last ounce of them.

If you only practice on old, used tires, it is impossible to expect to go out on new tires and get the very most out of them. Therefore, it is important to practice some of the time on new tires. And when you do, treat it just like a qualifying session.

You'll need to practice qualifying, whether on used or new tires. You must practice getting up to speed and laying down a great qualifying lap immediately. Whether your qualifying session is 2 laps or 20, your tires are going to have the most grip in the first two to four laps. You need to learn how to drive your kart at the limit within the first one or two laps.

Other than in some strange circumstances or when using an odd type of tire, typically you want to work as much heat into your tires as possible—as quickly as possible. This is especially true on a cold day. To do that, from the second you leave the pits you have to work the kart constantly on the warm-up lap, just pitching it back and forth, scrubbing the tires (also building heat in the engine).

Turning in the flying qualifying lap is perhaps more a matter of your mental preparation and state of mind than any other part of racing. You must be totally focused on the job at hand, ready to attack the circuit. Just don't drive way over your head or too aggressively, which will only cause you to go slower (and hurt your tires, which you will probably have to use in the race).

You need to have a clear mental picture of exactly how you are going to approach the qualifying session. Are you going to get out in front of everyone else and try to put in your time right away, or are you going to go out toward the end of the field and wait for the end of the session to put in your flyer? Does your kart handle better and have more grip with relatively cool tires, or do they need a lot of laps to get them to their peak operating temperature? Do you need to work at calming yourself down before qualifying, or do you need to crank up your intensity level? Do you want to see your lap times each lap, or do you drive faster if you don't know them until the end of the session?

These are all questions for which you need to discover the answers. What works for one driver and kart does not necessarily work for another. To be a great qualifier, you need to establish the routine that brings out the best in you and your kart, and then use it.

Race Starts

Race starts are probably the most dangerous part of a race, as this is when everyone is running closest together. The chance of getting your wheels tangled up with another kart's is at its highest on the opening lap or so. For this reason, it is important for you to have a game plan before the start. If your game plan is to make it safely through the first lap and then settle down to get to the front of the pack later, you may be less likely to have a big shunt than if your only goal is to get the lead before the first corner.

Regardless of your plan, it is unlikely you will win many kart races if you do not drive every second of the race flat out.

On the warm-up or pace lap before the start of the race, your primary objective is to get the tires and engine up to their ideal

Ninety percent of what it takes to qualify well is in your head. It's your mental approach to qualifying that will determine where you start the race. Develop a mental routine that gets you into the right state of mind for qualifying.

operating temperatures. With some very sticky tires you can actually get so much heat into them on the warm-up lap that you begin to pick up bits of rubber and dirt off the track. That is why you need to constantly work the tires, weaving back and forth, accelerating and braking hard. That should get them heated up and keep them clean at the same time. Be aware, though, that some karting clubs and sanctioning bodies do not allow weaving back and forth on the pace lap. Check the rule book.

Your first priority at the start, at least, is to hold your position, not letting anyone pass you. Your second priority is to gain positions. Again, with all the karts bunched up close together heading for turn one on the first lap, it's easy for two or more karts to interlock wheels and end up in a big crash. The best advice for avoiding this is to look as far ahead as possible. If there is a crash ahead of you, the farther up the track you are looking, the more time you will have to react—you may be able

Here's a typical race start, with karts bunched together in rows of two. The race starts either when the green flag falls, or when the karts ahead of you begin to accelerate. If you wait for the green flag, you may get left behind. *GO Racing Magazine*

to find a hole between karts to squirt through, or you may have to resort to taking to the dirt or grass at the side of the track. Whatever it takes to avoid the melee, do it.

Especially on the first lap, if you give an inch or back off for a second, you are most likely going to lose positions. Karts are so small and they can change directions so quickly that if you leave an opening, it is likely someone will dive in there and take the position from you.

Be proactive on the starts. There are a lot of positions, and time to be gained, and an awful lot to lose. Some drivers have the attitude that the race can't be won in the first corner, so the start is not that important. They think, "I'll just wait until we spread out, then I'll get going." That approach is fine if your goal is simply to have fun and be safe, but if you want to win at most levels of karting, you need to be more assertive. Remember, every other driver is going to "get going" too, and if they do it right off, you probably won't catch them.

This is especially true for short-heat races. In a 10-lap race, it doesn't matter how quick you are if you've given up too many positions at the start. There may not be enough time to make up what you've lost.

This is not an uncommon scene in the first turn of the first lap of a race. More crashes occur at this point in a race than at any other time. These drivers may be wishing they had taken the attitude of just getting cleanly through the first lap. *GO Racing Magazine*

Having said that, the old saying still applies: "To finish first, you first have to finish." It doesn't matter how many karts you either pass or hold off going into turn one; if you don't make it past the first lap, you will never win.

Races are started in one of two ways: rolling starts or standing starts. Either way, unless you are starting on the front row of the grid, remember this: the race really begins when the front-row karts begin to accelerate. If you wait for the start flag to be waved, you may get left behind. You must look ahead and watch for more than just the flag to be waved,

especially if you are starting back a ways on the grid. Watch the two karts on the front row. The instant they begin to accelerate, stand on the throttle.

That said, be sure you know and understand the rules where you are racing. In some forms of kart racing, jumping the start in any way means an immediate penalty. Taking that kind of risk may not be worth it.

Race Strategy

Once you are into the race, your strategy is pretty straightforward. Drive as fast as you can.

Although a good strategy for a race weekend may be to finish well in all your heat races to get a good starting position for the final, once you are in a kart race there is only one strategy: drive absolutely flat out as consistently as possible, lap after lap. If you do that and don't make any errors, you've got a chance of winning.

No matter what, no matter how much of a lead you have, never look back to see how well you are doing. Just continue to drive your own race. There is nothing you can do about your competition, anyway. The only thing you can affect is your own performance. If you think that you have a sizeable lead and back off even a little bit, there is a better chance you will make an error. Or, if you notice another kart or two right on your rear bumper, you may try too hard, get nervous, and make a mistake. Never, ever look back. Just focus on your own driving—being fast, precise, and consistent.

About the only time you ever should even think about pacing yourself in a kart race is if you are experiencing a problem with your kart, and your only objective now is simply to finish.

If you are chasing another kart that seems to be faster than you, do not back off, thinking, "I'm never going to catch him anyway." The more pressure you can keep on him, the better chance that he will make a mistake and hand you the position—or that his kart will break. Many times races have been won by drivers who have kept the pressure on and then been in position to take advantage of a competitor's problem. But you have to be close to do so. If you've backed off, you may be too far away to be rewarded with good luck.

Passing

There are three ways pass another kart:
- By driving around it in a corner;
- By out-accelerating it on a straightaway;
- By out-braking it on the approach to a corner.

By far the most difficult of these three options is the first one, passing another kart in a corner. The easiest, if your kart has a sufficient power advantage, is the second option. Of course, how well you drive the corner leading onto the straight is also a determining factor in being able to use this method. No matter how much of a power advantage your kart has over the competition, if you do not get a good acceleration run off of the corner, it will be difficult to pass. That is why your corner exit is so critical—so you can pass your competition and stop them from passing you.

The third option, out-braking another kart, is the most frequently used method of passing. If you are not good at the out-braking pass, you will never make a good racer. Perhaps the most important thing to remember in making this type of pass is that you do not have to get completely past the other kart. In fact, if you do, you have opened up an opportunity for the other driver to re-pass you on the exit of the turn. Unless you can get so far past the other kart that you can then move back over onto the ideal line before turning into the corner, your best bet is simply to get side by side with the other kart. That way, the only thing the driver can do is try to drive around the outside of you on the corner—which is unlikely to be successful—or wait until you have entered the turn, and then follow you at your speed. That does not give him a chance to re-pass you.

To make successful out-braking passes, obviously you have to be good at braking at the very last second for a corner. If you cannot brake as late for a turn as your competition, it will be next to impossible to pass him. Understand, though, that you do not have to brake as late as possible every lap. You only have to

Of all the ways to pass a competitor, this is typically the most difficult—around another kart in the middle of a corner. Unless you are significantly quicker than the other kart, the odds of executing this type of pass are not good because you have to travel farther in less time than your competitor.

If your kart has a power advantage, or you have a very good exit run off the previous corner, passing down the straightaway is the easiest overtaking maneuver you'll ever make.

The most common overtaking maneuver is outbraking another kart as you enter a corner. It often ends up in a competition to see who can begin braking the latest. It is also one of the easiest passes to defend, as all you have to do is move to the inside of the track to take the line away from the other driver.

This series of photos shows what happens when a kart carries too much speed into a corner when outbraking a competitor. You can see the kart on the inside at the entry of the corner slides wide toward the exit, and the other driver tucks back to the inside and re-passes.

do it once. But to do it that one time, you should at least have practiced it before the race. In fact, it is important to practice braking very late—and off-line—a number of times during practice so that you know just how deep you can go when attempting an out-braking pass. If you leave it until the race to try it for the first time, the chances of your getting it absolutely right are slim.

The most important rule when making any type of pass is to present yourself. What that means is make sure the other driver knows where you are. If you are making an out-braking pass, but you only get about one-half of the way up beside your competitor (where the nose of your kart is even with the seat of his), you are asking for him to turn into the corner in front of you. This "closing the door" or "chopping you off" often results in some type of contact between your kart and the competition.

To avoid this type of situation, you may have to ease up very slightly on the brakes for just a fraction of a second while braking—just enough to allow you to get right beside the other kart. That is as far up as you will ever need to be, as you now control the corner—and the other driver cannot possibly miss seeing you.

A common error that drivers make when out-braking a competitor is moving too far to the inside of the track. Let's say you are approaching a tight right-hand corner, following another kart. Just as you get to your braking point, you move to the right and dive down the inside, out-braking the other driver. Ideally, you should place your kart within a foot or so of the side of the other kart—not a kart or two's width away from it. There are a number of reasons for doing this.

First, it keeps your kart as close to the ideal line when turning into the corner as possible, meaning your exit speed will be affected as little

Here's the classic outbraking pass done right. The driver on the inside "presented" himself in a position where the other driver could see him but not be able to do anything about the pass. In other words, the passing driver took the line away from the other driver.

The driver passing on the inside has put himself in a bad position. Not only has he tightened up his line more than necessary (which may allow the other kart to re-pass him at the exit of the corner), but he is so far away from the other kart that it is difficult for the other driver to see him. He's almost asking to be hit.

The driver in the number 00 kart has done a great job of presenting himself to the other driver, getting his cart in a position to safely take the line away from the other kart. Just how far alongside another kart you have to be to take the line is one of those gray areas.

as possible. Second, it gives your competitor less room to maneuver into a position to attempt to re-pass you. Third, it is easier for the other driver to see you, reducing the chances of him turning into you. And finally, if you do have some contact with the other kart, there will be less momentum in the collision. If the other driver turns into you from several feet away, by the time he hits you he will have a fair bit of momentum, causing a bigger crash; if you are only a foot or less apart, you will probably just glance off of each other and carry on.

When you are trying to get past another kart in front of you, sometimes you may need to set up the overtaking move a few corners

Here's the same pass done right. The passing driver on the inside has presented himself—he is close enough to allow the other driver to see him—and taken the line away from the kart on the outside.

before actually making the pass. This is especially true if the driver in front of you is driving a defensive line in an attempt to block you. Usually the driver in this situation is keeping slightly to the inside on the approach to the corner. If you continue to drive the ideal line, you will be faster exiting the turn, therefore setting yourself up to make a decisive move at the next corner—one that, no matter how much the other driver blocks, cannot be defended.

Often, to set up this pass, you may actually have to hang back just slightly from the other kart so that your momentum is not interrupted by the other kart once you start accelerating. The trick is to time it just right so that you can accelerate hard out of the corner and slip past your competitor without his being able to do anything about it.

Passing in any type of kart should be premeditated. In other words, you need to plan ahead. If not, you will find yourself having to slow down more than necessary. Having said that, you will have a bit of room for error with the more powerful karts, including shifter karts and direct-drive two-stroke karts, where the power-to-weight ratio is relatively high. If you do have to slow down more than usual to make a pass, you have the engine power to regain your momentum.

If you are being passed, your number-one priority is to lose as little time as possible; the second is to see if there is a way you can re-pass. Always look for, and be prepared for, an opportunity to re-pass. Many drivers get so excited while making a pass that they make simple mistakes, often leaving the door open to get back around them.

With four-cycle karts, since they have less horsepower, you need careful planning to find the right opportunity and place to pass. The goal is to pass in a way that slows you down the least. You might be able to make the pass, but if you have to almost come to a stop doing it, you may get re-passed. It then takes you half a lap to regain all your momentum, and you've gone from fighting for the lead to running well back, all in the space of one lap.

Within reason, if you were racing a shifter kart, that pass may have been okay because you can just grab a lower gear and you're off and running again—the shifter's power allows you to regain your momentum more easily.

Sometimes a driver will set up a successful pass with a number of fakes. If you think that ultimately you can out-brake a competitor into a corner, but he aggressively defends the inside line, threaten him with an outside pass for a few laps. If it appears to him that you have a serious chance of getting by him on the outside, eventually he will move to block you there. The second he does that, you dive down the inside, and you're gone.

Being Passed

Although being passed is something no karter wants to be good at, the really good drivers do know how to let that happen without it costing them too much—especially without losing too much momentum. If it is imminent that you are going to be passed—that is, a kart behind you is significantly faster than you and it is only a matter of time before he passes you—your objective is to lose as little time as possible while this occurs.

It is not uncommon for a driver to move over a little to let a faster kart go by, only to have three or four other karts—often ones that were no faster—get by as well. That is why it is important not to make it too easy for the faster kart to pass. If you do, you will probably drive off-line, lose your own momentum, and hand a few positions over to your competitors. The key is to lose as little momentum and position as possible while letting the faster kart by.

How do you do that? The first thing to remember is that the faster kart is just that—faster than you. If he is that much faster, he will find a way past without your moving off the line too far. Second, he probably doesn't expect you to move out of the way for him. If you make an inconsistent move—one he isn't expecting—such as moving way off-line, that may be exactly where he was planning to go. In most cases, it is best to stay exactly on your normal line. That way, the faster driver knows what to expect.

If anything, you may just want to back off slightly earlier on the approach to a corner to allow him to easily out-brake you into the turn. That also allows you the opportunity to slip directly in behind him through the corner. You never know: by following him you might just learn something that could lead to your going faster.

It is not always a much faster kart that is able to pass you, or makes an attempt to pass you. Often, it is another competitor who is very closely matched with you in speed. That is what a good race is all about. Sometimes, if a closely matched competitor tries passing you, it

is best not to fight too hard to hold him off—sometimes. Once he begins his pass on you, you can occasionally benefit by letting him go and then re-passing him.

For example, if a competitor tries out-braking you into a hairpin turn, you have three options:

- You can let him go, fall in directly behind him, and hope to learn something from him (his cornering line that may help you go faster; where his weaknesses are so that you can re-pass him later in the race; and so on).
- You can fight him for the corner, trying to move over to "crowd" him as much as possible, while braking, and then try to drive around the corner on the outside of him, hoping to hold off the pass.
- You can let him make the pass, but set yourself up to immediately re-pass him. Usually, that means turning in a bit later than normal, aiming for a later apex, and getting back on the throttle earlier than your competitor, in hopes that you can out-accelerate him on the exit of the corner.

Which option you choose depends on what stage the race is in (if it is the last lap, for example, it will not do any good to choose the first option) and where you think your strengths and weaknesses are in comparison to him.

The Defensive Line

A defensive line not only slows up the kart that is trying to pass you, but you as well. Anytime you move off of the ideal line to protect your position, you will not be as fast. Perhaps the best way, then, to defend your position is not by driving a defensive line or blocking, but by focusing on your own line—by driving as quickly as you can on the ideal line. You may just find that you can actually

The driver of the number 2 kart is driving a defensive line, having moved to the inside to take the line away from the following kart. You can often get away with a defensive line for a lap or two, but after that you will probably have lost so much speed and momentum that the other driver will find some way around you. You will also have lost ground to other karts ahead of and behind you.

pull away slightly from your competitors, rather than fighting them off.

Having said that, there are times when you will want to make it as difficult as possible—within reason—for a competitor to pass you. For example, if another kart is catching you, and you only have a lap or two left in the race, you shouldn't just pull over and let him pass you. Instead, you want to drive a consistent line that leaves little room for anyone to get by.

Notice we said "consistent" in that last sentence. Let's make one thing clear here. There is a world of difference between driving a defensive line and blocking. A defensive line means driving your kart on a line that makes it difficult to pass. Blocking usually involves moving back and forth across the track more

than once. If you have to resort to outright blocking to maintain a position, you probably don't deserve the position. Work on making your kart and your driving faster, and then you won't have to rely on blocking to get you the position. Most important, realize that blocking is dangerous—it can get you and your competitors hurt.

If you have to make more than one move to keep another kart behind you, that's blocking. Weaving from one side of the track to the other and back again—blocking—will probably result in someone getting hurt. It will often result in getting you penalized, as well. If you make *one* move, from one side of the track to the other, though, that is driving a defensive line.

The bottom line is that driving a defensive line is not always appropriate. There is a time and place for it, such as the last lap or two of a race, but you really have to think about whether you want to hold a position by doing something that is sometimes looked upon as a cheap, desperate move. You also need to think about whether you want a reputation as a driver who resorts to blocking, and what that will mean to your driving career and/or your enjoyment level. There is is a very fine line between driving a defensive line and blocking, and your perception of what you are doing may differ from other people's perception. And you know what they say about perception—it is reality.

So, let's say it is the last lap of a race and you are trying to keep a kart that is just slightly faster than you behind. How do you do that? By never leaving any more than a kart's width between your kart and the inside edge of the track. To a competitor trying to get by you, that amount of room does not look very inviting. Instead, it looks like a disaster waiting to happen, and most drivers will shy away from diving down the inside of you entering a turn. And, of course, trying to pass you on the outside is less inviting—and less likely to be successful.

By driving this kind of line, hugging toward the inside of the turn, you will definitely be slower over an entire lap. Any competitor ahead of you will likely pull further ahead. But unless the kart behind you is much faster, you will probably be able to maintain your position for a short time.

Driving a defensive line requires driving a tighter radius around the corners, which, as you know, means you will have to drive slower than if you were driving the ideal line. That probably means using the brakes more than you would normally. Fortunately, if you are in front and

Turning your head and looking over your shoulder to see another kart most often results in your getting passed. You need to learn to "feel" the karts behind you, perhaps catching just a brief glimpse of them, or hearing them, as you enter tight turns.

taking up most of the best part of the track surface, it will be difficult for anyone to get by you. The competitor is going to have to follow you through the corner in hopes of passing you on the straightaway, or in the next corner.

When you have a competitor right on your tail, one of the most difficult things to resist is looking behind you. Any amount of time you spend looking over your shoulder is time and attention not put into going faster. Many times, if the driver would only focus as much attention on his own driving as he does on looking over his shoulder, he would be miles ahead. Knowing exactly where a kart is behind you rarely makes any real difference. Wait until you can hear, or even feel, the kart behind you. If you can't hear or feel the kart, it probably isn't close enough to get by you anyway—that is, if you are focusing on driving your own kart, and not his.

Once you look over your shoulder, your competitor knows he's got you. If he sees you looking back, he will be more likely to take a

This is what it looks like from the middle of a pack of karts, all battling for position. Of course, your goal is to have only open track in front of you! *GO Racing Magazine*

bigger chance to pass you, since he knows you are spending more time focused on him than on the track in front of you. Of course, keep that in mind when you are following another driver.

Don't worry about the competitors behind you. The only karts you need to think about are the ones in front of you and beside you.

Obviously, in a kart, you don't have mirrors. You can hear the other kart, but you don't really know where he is. You know he's close, but you just have to shut him out and drive your own race.

Good kart racers are good at knowing where other people are without the use of mirrors. When they start racing cars, they have this awareness of other cars around them that other racers never get. They're great in

traffic, because they haven't had mirrors to rely on. After you've been racing karts for some time, you get this sixth sense of where other people are around you.

Traffic

Passing and being passed gets even trickier when there are more than two karts involved. Even so, keep the main objectives in mind. Number one, you want to spend as little time passing another kart as possible. And second, if you are being passed, you also want to lose as little time as possible.

If you are in the middle of a pack of karts trying to make a pass on several ahead of you, you need to watch that you don't get blocked in and end up losing a spot or two to the karts following. There are times when you are going to have to pull out to begin a pass before you are really ready to do so. The reason is to keep the kart directly in front of you from making a move before you do.

If there are a few karts directly behind you, and one pulls out to pass you, your goal is to make sure you do not get forced off your line to the point that a train of karts gets by, with you losing multiple positions. If the kart directly behind you goes to the inside, make it very clear to the other karts behind you that you intend to slot back in line once he has gotten by. That means not pulling to the outside edge of the track. Instead, run as close as possible to the kart passing you. That doesn't leave any room for another kart to make a move, and lets him know your intentions.

Of course, if one kart does dive down the inside of you on the approach to a corner, expect and be ready for another to follow. Many crashes have been caused by a driver who thought there was only one kart passing him, who then turned in to the corner once it was past only to slam into the second kart making the same overtaking move.

There may be times when you are just not as fast as the other karts on the track. That may be because your kart is not competitive or you lack experience. Either way, it is best not to block or hold up the faster karts, for a couple of reasons. First, at that stage you will probably learn more by letting a faster kart by and following—observing what the other driver is doing to go so fast. And second, if you get a reputation as a driver who either is unaware or is a blocker, it can make racing difficult for a long time. If that happens, you can only hope the race officials take some action

This photo demonstrates what often happens when a number of karts all head into a corner together. As the front kart begins braking, the line of karts behind begins to stack up and someone gets hit in the rear, sending karts in every direction. Unless you are the first or second kart in a line, you may have to brake a little earlier than usual to avoid running into the back of another kart. *GO Racing Magazine*

against you, because if not, some drivers will decide to teach you a lesson—a hard lesson.

If you are running behind a number of karts, as you begin braking when approaching a corner you must be prepared for the karts in front of you to "stack up." For example, imagine six karts in row. As the first kart applies his brakes to slow for a corner, the second kart in line cannot go quite as deep because the kart in front has already started to slow down, so he must brake just slightly earlier than normal. Therefore, the third kart in line must do the same, and so on down the line. If you are the sixth kart in line, you will either have to brake earlier than normal, or move to the inside and make a pass.

Despite the need for the driver to go into each race with the strategy to drive as fast as possible for the whole race, there is a place for patience. When racing a kart, you are most often running nose to tail. There may be 25 karts and it's hard to pass on some of the circuits. The guy who's twenty-fifth is still a really good kart racer, but unless someone makes a

A kart has just spun in front of you; what do you do? Start by not looking at it. Look for the opening, most often to the inside. Rarely will a kart spin to the inside, or to where it has already been.

mistake, he's not going to get by. He might force his way past, but a lot of times you just can't get by someone. So you have to learn patience. Drive as fast as you can, pass whenever you can, but know that it is the last lap that decides the final positions. Make sure you are there at the end.

Contact and Crashes

Hitting another kart on purpose is definitely not on the recommended to-do list. Any time two karts touch, there is a very good chance that they will interlock tires, sending one or both of them flying in the air. Many drivers have been seriously hurt doing this.

Now, not all drivers follow this advice. Some drivers will try to force you out of their way to slow you down and get past you. Keep this in mind: you are always better to be the

hitter than the hittee. In other words, if a competitor is about to push you off-line or off the track, push back first. Whoever initiates the contact will have the momentum, and will probably come away least affected. Of course, race officials are always watching for excessive contact, and if you are seen as the driver who initiated a pushing match, you will be penalized. That is why it is best to stay away from contact altogether, although there are times where it cannot be avoided. And that is when you need to be prepared to be the hitter.

Anytime you bump another kart from behind you give it an extra burst of acceleration and hurt your momentum. With this in mind, some drivers will actually delay their acceleration or ease up slightly, hoping another kart will give them a little nudge. We believe the odds of getting that maneuver just

The key to avoiding a spinning kart is to look away from it, concentrating on where you want to go, not where you don't want to go. If you look at the spinning kart, you will steer toward it.

right are not nearly as good as gaining on your competition by focusing on driving as quickly as possible on your own.

With all this in mind, always remember that karting is supposed to be a non-contact sport.

When it comes to avoiding another kart that is spinning, there are no definite rules. It is next to impossible to predict all the possible scenarios that could occur. If there is a rule of thumb—a guess you might take when a guess is as good as you'll get—it's to head toward the spinning kart. Why? Because it is very rare for a spinning kart to spin back to where it once was. Heading for the back of the kart is

also good advice. Since many karts do not have clutches, the likelihood of one rolling backward is not very high.

If there is a collision between a number of karts, the most important thing is to look for the hole, or gap, in the traffic. Although that sounds like obvious advice, actually doing it is not as easy as it seems. Human nature tends to make our eyes focus on objects more easily than on nothing—that is, on the karts instead of the gap. When there is a problem in front of you, your eyes will be attracted to the problem. And wherever you look is where you're going to drive. So you need to practice looking for the gap in traffic—looking at nothing.

7

Using Your Head

In chapter 2 we stated that the most important component of your kart—the main thing that determines whether you win or lose—is your tires. Let us update that. The thing that has the biggest effect on whether you win or lose is you, and specifically, your mind.

Vision

Vision is everything, whether you are driving a kart, a car on the street, a truck, a Formula One car, or anything else. Where you look, and what you are aware of, is the key to being successful.

We talked earlier in the book about how everything you do with the kart should be done as smoothly as possible. Knowing how far ahead and where to look is the number-one key to driving smoothly.

One of the biggest differences between great drivers—whether on the street, driving race cars, or karts—and the not-so-great is how far ahead they focus their vision. Great drivers look far ahead. By doing that, they have more time to react. With more time to react, everything they do is done more smoothly. Looking farther ahead allows you to act, rather than

react. It is more of a planned action, rather than a panicked reaction.

If your vision is focused just a short distance in front of your kart, you will find yourself having to make many quick adjustments on the steering wheel to get the kart to go where you want. If you are focused well ahead instead, your steering inputs will be smooth, subtle, and positive—you will steer exactly where you want to go.

How far ahead should you be looking? As far as possible. In karting, there is no general rule like there is when driving on the street. On the street, it is recommended you look at least 12 seconds ahead. The idea is to pick a point up ahead on the road where you are focusing your vision, and begin counting "one-thousand-one, one-thousand-two", and so on. If you've been looking far enough ahead, your car will be passing that point at about the time you are counting "one-thousand-twelve."

Unfortunately, there is not a simple formula like this that you can follow on the race track. If you ever tried this at karting speed, you would be crashing off the track before you had a chance to count to "one-thousand-two."

The real key to success in kart racing is what's inside your helmet.

Of course if you practice looking at least 12 seconds ahead when driving on the street, you will get into the habit of looking far ahead, and that will help on the race track.

Your goal is to look far enough ahead that you do not feel rushed at any point on the track, and that you are aware of what is going on ahead of you. As you exit one corner, you should already be looking for the braking and turn-in points for the next corner. By the time you are braking for the corner, you should be looking through the turn-in point and toward the apex. While turning in for the corner, you should be looking through the apex and seeing the exit of the corner. Around the apex, you

should be looking through the exit point and down the next straightaway.

Not only are you looking far ahead, but you are thinking far ahead.

The farther ahead you look, the slower everything appears to be coming at you. If it feels as though everything is happening too fast to keep up with, you are not looking far enough ahead.

As you drive down the straightaway approaching a corner, look for the turn-in point well before you get to it. Before you get to the turn-in point, turn your head and find the apex; before you get to the apex, look through the turn and find the exit; and so on.

The farther ahead you look, the smoother and faster you will drive. Practice looking well down the track. Keep reminding yourself of this.

The bottom line is that you need to stay at least one step ahead of where you are. If you look just in front of the kart, you will see things coming at you too fast, and you will not be smooth.

This technique—looking far ahead—is why some drivers seem to be able to avoid any type of crashing or spinning kart in front of them, while other drivers seem to be attracted to them like a magnet. When you are looking far ahead, you have time to see the trouble ahead and to decide what to do about it.

Have you ever been walking toward another person in a hallway or on a sidewalk, and as you get closer you move to the right, so does the other person; you move to the left, and

he or she does the same—and you practically bump into each other, or at least have to stop walking. Why does that happen? Because you are looking at each other.

Our brains are "wired" in such a way that we move toward what we look at. Focus your eyes on something, and it is like a magnet—it draws you toward it. People do it all the time driving on the highway: they look off to the side of the road to admire some scenery, and the car follows—oftentimes onto the shoulder of the road.

Wherever you look is where the kart will go. So look where you want to go, not where you don't want to go. Typically that means looking far down the track, but if you want

Well before a corner, you need to see your braking and turn-in points, and look through the turn toward the apex. The sooner you begin planning how you are going to attack a corner, the better job you will do.

the kart to run past an apex area of a corner, focus your eyes there and the kart will follow. If you want to hit the space between a tangle of karts, that's where you have to look. If you focus your eyes off to the side of the track, where you think you may go off, you will find a way of getting there!

Most people seem to think that a person either has good eyesight or doesn't. They also seem to resign themselves to the "fact" that as you get older your vision deteriorates. And yet these same people will admit that exercising their bodies will maintain their health into old age. If that theory works for the rest of your body—and it does—why shouldn't it for your eyesight?

Although it has a physical and hereditary component, good vision is also a learned sense. That is, with practice, you can improve your vision. That is why, if you want to be a good kart racer, we recommend some form of vision therapy. There are sports vision therapists in most large cities who can give you a variety of vision exercises to improve and maintain the health of your eyesight for years to come. Be aware, though, that many doctors, ophthalmologists, and optometrists do not believe in vision therapy. Their business is helping you deal with failing vision by getting you to wear glasses. You may be able to get a referral to a vision therapist from one of these, or you may have to do the research yourself to

The driver in this photo is clearly looking toward the exit of the turn. Perfect!

find one. There are a few good books on the market about vision therapy, as well.

Crashes are often blamed on a driver making a bad decision on the race track. He may have tried a pass that didn't have a hope in you-know-what of being successful; or he may have tried taking a corner flat out that he had never come close to taking at that speed before. These so-called bad decisions result in some type of crash, and the driver earns a reputation for making bad decisions.

Often, the real cause for these crashes is not a matter of making a bad decision. The real cause is a lack of good-quality sensory input upon which to base the decision. For example, if the driver's vision is restricted in even the slightest way, what looks like a good opportunity to pass is really a crash waiting to happen. You see, it is not a problem with the driver's decision-making abilities, it's a problem with his vision and the information that comes with it.

You want your mind to receive as much high-quality sensory input as possible. That information, along with the sensory input from your sense of feel and hearing, will allow

Practically everything you do behind the wheel of your kart is a result of the information your eyes send to your brain. Practice being aware of everything around you so that your eyes send as much information as possible to your brain. The more information you have, the better your line, decisions, and overall driving performance will be.

you to make good decisions and direct your body to activate the appropriate physical action (turn the steering wheel, ease off the brake pedal, squeeze the throttle, and so on).

If you want to be a successful kart racer, you owe it to yourself to establish a regular routine of vision exercises. Perhaps the best place to begin is by reading Ross Bentley's and Ronn Langford's book, *Inner Speed Secrets*. They provide you with a number of vision exercises that are specifically designed to improve your racing performance.

Visualization

It doesn't matter whether you are driving a kart, playing golf, or playing the piano; if you can't do it in your mind, you will never do it physically.

Your mind is an amazing and very powerful tool. But it can be "fooled" into believing something is real when it is just imagined. For example, take a few moments to close your eyes, breathe deeply and slowly, and relax. Then, imagine a bright yellow lemon. Imagine picking that lemon up in your hands and

This driver is taking a few moments to close his eyes and visualize a driving technique; he's practicing it mentally prior to heading onto the track to physically do it. It is a waste of time and money to go onto a race track without having taken the time to plan and practice in your mind what you intend to do.

feeling its surface, noticing its dimples, the texture of the skin. In your mind, see yourself picking up a knife and cutting the lemon in half, seeing the juice dripping from the face of it, and then bringing one-half of the lemon up to your nose and smelling it. Now, lick it.

What happened when you did that? Did your mouth begin to fill with saliva? For most people it does, but why? You didn't actually have citric acid from the lemon in your mouth, but your mind thought you did. And that triggered a reaction.

The same thing occurs in the kart. If you can imagine exactly what you want to do on the race track, your mind will trigger the correct and appropriate physical action to accomplish it.

You can use this to your advantage. You can use your imagination to learn faster. This technique is often referred to as visualization. The problem with visualization is that it only uses one of your senses—your vision. If you use your hearing and sense of feel in addition to vision, by imagining the sound and feel of your driving, it will be even more

Staying focused and keeping your concentration levels up can sometimes be more challenging once you get in the lead and no longer have anyone in front of you with whom to pace yourself. This is when you really need a preplanned "trigger" to switch on the concentration. *Go Racing*

section of the track, you need to spend time practicing that section of track. In other words, if you have a blank section of track mentally, you will not be fast through that section.

If you cannot do something in your mind, you will never be able to do it on the track. The opposite is also true: if you can do something mentally, you can do it physically—if you use actualization. Spend time actualizing before and after driving your kart. The more you do it, the better you will get at it, and the better a kart racer you will be.

Focus and Concentration

There is no doubt that it takes a tremendous amount of concentration to drive a kart. Mentally, you must be prepared to think only of the job at hand—driving. If your mind is thinking about something besides the proper braking and turn-in points, apexes, picking up the throttle at the right time, being smooth, and so on, it's not only going to reflect in your lap times; it may also be dangerous to you and other drivers on the track.

Most people would agree that focus and concentration are critical to winning kart races. And yet, most drivers do very little to improve their ability to concentrate.

effective. Think of it as actualization, rather than visualization.

Ultimately, you should be able to close your eyes and imagine—actualize—yourself driving around the race track at speed, while using a stopwatch to time your mental lap, and be within a second of your real lap time. If you have problems imagining a certain

No matter how many karts are surrounding you, focus on your own performance and driving. The driver who does that best most often ends up in the lead. Remember, there is only one kart and driver you have control over. *GO Racing Magazine*

If you find yourself losing concentration at any point in a practice or qualifying session, or the race, you need to work at developing the ability to hold your focus for a longer period of time. So, how do you do that? You could do that simply through more practice, and that would help. In fact, by practicing driving for longer periods of time

than your races will ever be, you can stretch your ability to concentrate. Our suggestion would be to practice driving for at least twice the length of the race.

Using the actualization technique that we just mentioned is another method of improving your focus. It is also very effective. By practicing mentally for lengths of time longer than your races, you will have made concentrating a habit. Start a stopwatch when you begin to actualize. At any time, when you begin to think of anything else, make note of the time. Continue to practice this until you can actualize for at least the length of your races.

While actualizing, if you do lose concentration, say the word "focus," and then see yourself getting right back into a high level of concentration again. What you are doing is building a trigger—a word that triggers an action. In this case, if you mentally practice having the word "focus" trigger you back into a state of full concentration, you will have programmed your mind to do that. Then, whenever you lose your concentration for a second on the track, you can say the word "focus" to yourself, and you will regain your concentration immediately—rather than focusing on the fact that you've lost your concentration!

Playing other sports, or video games, that require a high level of concentration for a long period of time is good practice for racing karts. To make video games really useful, though, you have to go into it with the same mental attitude that you do with your kart racing. If you play them too casually, not concerned about whether you lose your focus or not, you will get very good at driving that way. If you practice losing your concentration, you will be good at losing your concentration.

Competition

Racing is all about competition. We would suggest, however, that if you focus on your own performance, and not on that of your competition, you will be more likely to win.

Many people in all forms of racing spend an awful lot of time and effort watching their competition, trying to figure out what they are doing—both on and off the track. If these people would put that much focus and attention into their own performance, they would most likely be so far ahead that they would not have to worry about the competition.

A perfect example of this is the driver who spends most of the time looking over his shoulder, watching for a competitor behind him. What happens, of course, is that because the driver is spending so much attention on what's going on behind him, he doesn't spend enough on what's in front. Therefore, he isn't as fast as he could be, and the competitor who was following not only catches him, but probably passes as well. If the first driver had expended the same energy on finding the ideal line and driving it as fast as possible, he likely would have held the other driver off—perhaps long enough to win the race.

Truth is, you really can't do anything about your competition. The only thing you have any control over is yourself. When you focus on your own performance, rather than on the competition or on winning, you have your best chance to win.

8
Safety

Overall, karting is one of the safest forms of motorsport. This is due to two factors: the relative speed of the karts and the safety equipment standards and rules that most clubs and sanctioning bodies enforce. Compared to race cars, karts are slow enough that if something should go wrong—and it does on a fairly regular basis—drivers are usually not seriously injured.

Of course, any time you drive a vehicle at or near its limit, there is a serious risk of getting hurt. This is especially so when the vehicles, like karts, have exposed wheels. For that reason, your attention to the quality, care, and use of your safety equipment is critical.

A kart's lower relative speed, compared to other types of race vehicles, is one of the reasons some drivers do not put enough attention into their safety equipment. They conclude that they are just not likely to get hurt at 30, 50, or 70 miles per hour—besides, it's not very macho to be worried about safety. Well, we will tell you how badly you can get hurt in karting. Very badly! To believe otherwise is some of the most flawed thinking in the history of motorsport. Imagine opening the door of a car traveling at

30 miles per hour and jumping out. You wouldn't do it, would you?

Our point, of course, is that karting is risky business, and you had better take safety seriously if you want to continue to enjoy it. Some people don't hesitate for a second to jump into a kart with only a helmet, and often not a good helmet. If you cannot afford good-quality safety equipment, if you can't afford even one part of it, you cannot afford to go racing.

Helmet

The old saying, "If your head is worth $10, then wear a $10 helmet," still applies. The helmet is probably the most important piece of safety equipment. After all, it protects your head, which protects your brain. Mess that up and you'll make a negative impact on much more than your karting future. Do not scrimp on the purchase of your helmet.

When buying a helmet, be careful to check for the Snell approval sticker inside, usually under the padding. If the helmet does not have this sticker, do not buy it. The rule book that you must conform to while

Although karting is relatively safe, crashes do happen—so be fully equipped and prepared.

competing will state that your helmet must be Snell approved. If you have a helmet that is not Snell approved, you will not be able to race.

The Snell Foundation, which was established in the late 1950s, tests and sets standards for helmets that manufacturers must meet. These standards are updated every five years. As of the writing of this book, most rule books state that your helmet must meet or exceed the Snell 95 standards (these standards will be changing soon). That means that if your helmet is Snell 90 approved, you will not be able to race with it.

The Snell certification on a helmet is a sign that it meets the latest standards for:

- Impact management—this tests how well it protects against impacts with other objects.
- Extent of protection—how much of your head is protected.
- Retention system strength—how well the chinstrap holds the helmet on your head.

The Bell Dominator is one of the best money can buy. Wear only the best helmet, and take care of it.

- Helmet positional stability—how much the helmet moves around on your head.

It should be obvious that an open-face helmet is totally unacceptable for karting.

If you chose a quality, brand-name helmet, and it has the latest Snell approval sticker inside, you know you have the best protection you can get. At the Bondurant School we use only Bell helmets, which meet the highest safety standards and which we feel are unsurpassed for driver protection.

Many drivers, particularly those who are new to the sport, will buy a used helmet from someone who is either quitting or upgrading to a newer helmet. This isn't a good idea because you don't know the history of a used helmet. If the helmet suffered structural damage in a crash, even damage that may not be apparent on visual inspection, it will not provide you with full protection. Also, the seller may not have taken good care of the helmet. Scratches, a worn strap, loose face shield, or damaged ventilation system could make the helmet uncomfortable or unsafe. Unless you know the history of a helmet and can see that it is in perfect condition, don't buy it.

Remember too that the helmet must fit properly. A top-quality helmet that doesn't fit correctly may not be any better than wearing one of those biker half-helmets. This is a common problem with young kart racers. Buying a helmet that a 10-year-old can grow into is asking for trouble. Parents who don't care enough about their child's safety to provide proper-fitting equipment should not be involved in motorsport.

A helmet should not be able to move around on your head. If you can rotate it side to side, or up and down, it is not tight enough. It should be as snug as possible, without being uncomfortable. If you are not used to wearing a helmet, even a proper-fitting helmet will feel slightly uncomfortable. It is all a matter of getting used to the feel. After purchasing a new helmet, we suggest you wear it around your house for long periods of time to get comfortable with it and discover any pressure points. Obviously, you want to discover these before you're in the middle of a race.

If a helmet does cause some pain from a pressure point, you should probably try another model or brand of helmet. Each model and brand has a slightly different fit, and as everyone's head is not the same shape, it may be necessary to try a number of helmets before deciding on the right one for you. Take the time to make sure your helmet fits properly and is comfortable.

Suit

Many drivers race without a full karting suit. They wear jeans and a jacket that offers some protection. That's okay if you don't care about your legs and knees as much as you do the rest of your body. For maximum protection, though, you should wear a full karting suit.

The main benefit of a karting suit is that it is designed to not rip open if you are tumbling down the track surface. The material actually

A proper karting suit will go a long way toward protecting you should you get thrown from the kart. Purpose-made karting suits are the only way to go.

allows you to slide on the asphalt, reducing the chances of your kneecap or elbow being ground into the pavement.

Some karting suits are a two-piece affair; others are one piece. The one-piece suits are much safer. The problem with two-piece suits is that it is easy for them to separate, exposing your body's midsection when you're thrown from your kart in a crash.

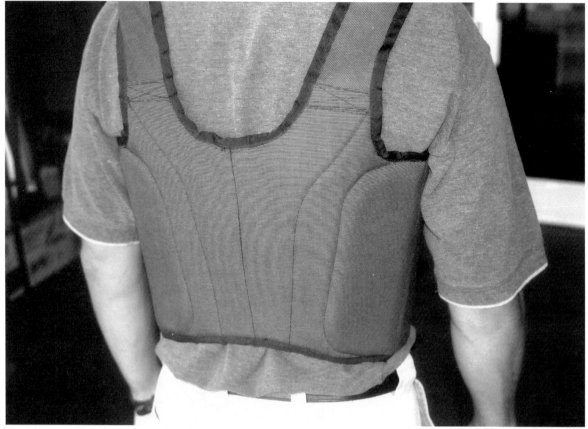

Most kart racers have at one time bruised or cracked some ribs. They will tell you that it is one of the most painful injuries you can ever experience and that a rib protector such as this is a must.

Make sure that you always wear a neck collar that is the right size for you, such as one of these.

Rib Protector

Using a rib protector is typically a matter of taste—it is not in the rule book. Perhaps it should be, though. With the g-forces your body experiences, especially in any type of crash, it is very easy for your ribs to be broken, or at least badly bruised. Both injuries are very painful.

The only way to protect yourself is to wear a rib protector. Most protectors are made of a high-impact plastic, covered with some type of material, and are worn under your suit. It is recommended that you wear a T-shirt under the rib protector, so that is does not rub and chafe against your skin.

Without proper racing shoes, much of the throttle and brake pedal sensitivity that we've talked about in this book is lost. Also, note how they cover the driver's ankles, providing much-needed protection.

Collar

In most clubs and sanctioning bodies, neck collars are mandatory. If it is not mandatory where you race, it should be. The neck collar's main role is to stop your helmet from impacting and breaking your collarbone in a crash. They can also help protect your neck from overextension injuries to some degree.

Ensure that you only use a neck collar that goes all the way around your neck and is fastened with Velcro. U-shaped neck collars without a Velcro fastener can fall off too easily.

Shoes

Go watch a kart race and you will see drivers wearing just about every variety of shoe, from hiking boots and running shoes to proper driving shoes. There is a reason why successful karters wear real driving shoes, and it is not just to look good. They provide better protection, particularly over the ankles, and give better feel on the pedals.

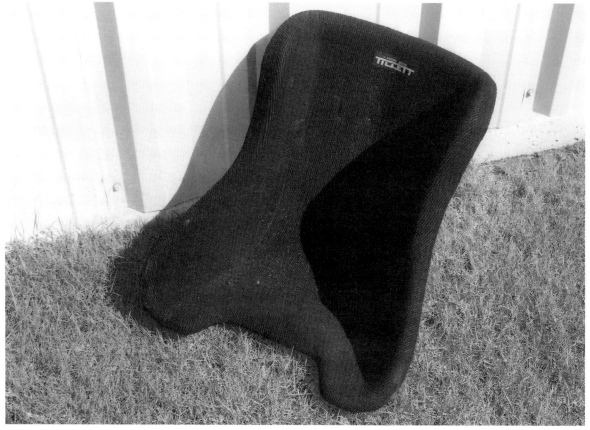

A well-fitted seat does much more than just make you comfortable (although that is important). It keeps you attached to the kart and provides a lot of feedback that allows you to drive the kart at the limit.

Gloves

Gloves serve two purposes. First, they give you better grip on the steering wheel and protect you from getting blisters. Second, they protect your hands if you are thrown from the kart and are sliding along the pavement.

Next to your helmet, gloves may be the most important piece of safety equipment you use. Preferably, you should use gloves specially designed for karting, for they are better at protecting your hands from road rash should you be thrown out of your kart in a crash.

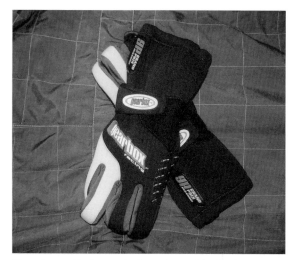

Use gloves that are designed specifically for karting, as they provide the best grip on the wheel and protection in case of a crash.

Here's a driver fitted snugly in his seat, wearing a rib protector over his suit. *Go Racing*

Seat

Why would we include the seat in this chapter on safety? In cars, what is one of the most important safety devices? Seatbelts. Well, karts do not have seatbelts, but they do have a seat thats job is to keep you safely attached to the kart. In fact, along with helping transmit the forces from the kart to your body, this is the seat's primary purpose. If you are moving around in relationship to the kart, not only will you not be receiving the necessary feedback, you will have to support your body by holding onto the steering wheel. This requires more effort on your part; it reduces your sense and feel of the kart, and it is unsafe.

Thinking of the seat as your seatbelt helps you determine just how snug-fitting it should be, and how it should support your body. The better it holds you in the kart, the better it protects you.

Kart seats can be purchased in a variety of shapes and sizes, so it is important that you spend the time to find one that matches your body. If you cannot find one that fits perfectly and holds you snugly, you may need to modify one by taping some foam in place. Do not worry about padding the seat, though. In fact, the less padding between you and the seat, the more feedback you will receive. On the other hand, if you are in agony from a part of the seat digging into your body, padding may be the only cure.

9
Kart Tuning

This is a driving book, not one about kart maintenance and tuning. So why do we have a chapter on kart tuning? Two reasons. First, an understanding of the basics of tuning your kart will make you a better driver. The more you understand about the handling characteristics, the chassis dynamics, tires, and engine tuning, the better you will be at adapting your driving to suit the kart.

Second, we want you to focus your efforts on driving the kart, not trying to get it to run or handle properly. So if we can give you enough of the basics to get your kart in good shape, the easier it will be to concentrate on your driving.

One of the best things about karting is the fact that you can, and should, work on your own kart. In some forms of car racing, the technology and time demands of preparing and tuning the car far exceed the capabilities of someone focused on driving. But that is not the case with karts. In fact, the more you know about the preparation and tuning of your kart, the better a driver you will be.

A key to being a great driver is having a great sense and feel for what the kart is

telling you. The better you understand the mechanical functions of your kart, the more sensitive you will be, and the better driver you will be.

Understand that what we are presenting in this chapter really are just the basics. To learn more, your best bet is to spend time talking to and observing someone who has been preparing and tuning karts successfully for years. No matter where you live, you should be able to find such a person.

Chassis

Ironically, getting a kart's chassis setup just right is so difficult because of the simplicity of the chassis. There is very little you can work with. So what you do with the few adjustments you have is critical. If you have come from racing cars to racing karts, many of the adjustments will seem backward and counterintuitive.

When it comes to setting up and adjusting a kart—as is the case with practically everything else—there is only one rule that never gets broken. And that rule is: all rules can, and will, be broken. In other words, just when you think there is a very specific set of rules that

Your entire karting experience will be more enjoyable and successful if you ensure your kart is properly prepared.

dictates exactly what you should adjust for every handling problem you may face, along comes a situation where the opposite of what is supposed to work solves the problem.

Perhaps the most important thing for you to understand is why each of the adjustments usually provides the resultant change in handling. If you truly understand why and how a change affects the kart, you will be able to adapt the suggested changes to suit your specific situation.

In terms of handling, your kart will do one of three things: it will oversteer, it will understeer, or it will be neutral handling. To accurately tune your kart's handling, you must first determine which of these three characteristics it has, to what degree, where it is displaying them, and what you as the driver are doing at the time. In addition, your kart may not have enough grip, or it can actually have too much grip.

To properly analyze your kart, be sure to debrief after every session on the track. Ask yourself some questions, such as, "Is the kart understeering or oversteering in the first third of the corner? Second third? Last third? Am I on the brakes, on the throttle, or transitioning between the two at the time? Am I turning the steering wheel, holding it still, or unwinding it?" Your objective is to fully understand

Getting just the right setup on your chassis—the ideal compromise between alignment, front and rear track, rear axle and chassis stiffness, and tire compound and pressures—can make a dramatic difference in cornering speeds. However, it is rare that you will ever have your kart handle perfectly in every corner. Therefore, you will need to learn how to adapt your driving to suit the way your kart handles.

exactly what the kart is doing, and why. If you know what it's doing and why, then you can find a solution; if you do not, it is very difficult to find a cure to a problem you do not fully understand.

Once you have determined what the kart is doing and what you would like to improve, then comes the time to begin tuning the chassis. The basic philosophy of tuning a kart chassis comes down to changing the amount of load that is transferred from the inside tires to the outside tires, and the bias from front to

rear. In simpler terms, do you want more grip on the front or rear?

Recall that a kart has a solid rear axle, and that one of your main ways to get around a corner quickly is to unload the inside rear tire to allow the kart to rotate. Changing whether your kart oversteers or understeers often comes down to changing the degree of unloading of the inside rear tire.

For example, if your kart is understeering, it may be that the inside rear tire is not being unloaded enough, resulting in the solid rear

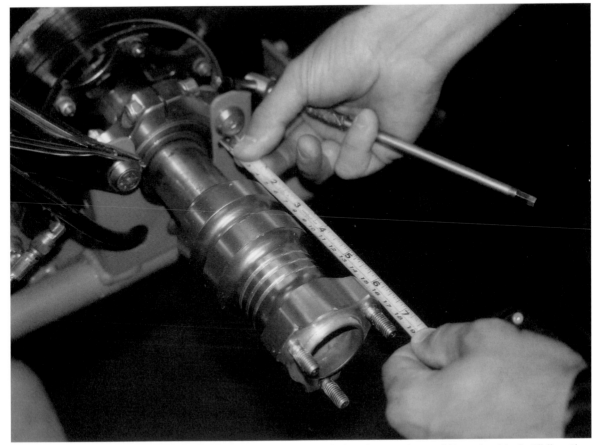

Here's a driver measuring the distance between the rear axle bearing carrier and the wheel hub. Sliding the wheel hub closer or farther from the bearing alters the rear track and the flexibility of the axle, and is one of the most effective chassis-tuning tools.

axle tending to drive the kart straight ahead. Your goal then is simply to make changes to help unload the inside rear tire more. To do that, you could do one of the following:

• Move the seat forward;
• Widen the rear track;
• Install a softer, more flexible rear axle;
• Increase the front castor.

With an understeering kart, you could also take a different approach, one designed to increase the grip of the front tires. In this case, you might try widening the front track.

If, on the other hand, your kart over-steers too much, your goal is to increase the load on the outside rear tire to increase its level of traction. To do that, you could do one of the following:

• Raise the seat height;
• Move the seat farther back;
• Narrow the rear track;
• Install a stiffer rear axle.

Again, you can use another approach, this time narrowing the front track to reduce its grip or traction.

This photo shows one seat brace, the chrome strut between the seat, and the chassis. By adding or removing struts, you change the chassis stiffness and the amount of load the driver places on the outside rear tire in a corner. This will increase or decrease the amount of rear tire traction.

For every rule there is an exception to the rule. Although these suggestions will work most of the time—with most karts, and with most drivers—they will not work all of the time. And these are not all of the adjustments that are possible to cure your handling problem. If you really think about, and understand, why these adjustments work, you will be better prepared to deal with the exceptions to the rules.

There are many other "tools"—adjustments—you can use to get your kart to handle the way you want. But since this is a driving book, and an entire book could be written on these adjustments alone, we are not going to get into the details of when and how they should be used. Some other tuning tools you can use, though, are adding or removing chassis strut bars, adjusting the

chassis torsion bars, changing to wheels with different stiffness characteristics, altering the camber of the front wheels, and so on.

The rules for altering the handling of a kart are as follows:

- To increase the grip of the rear tires (to reduce oversteer), increase the transfer of weight/load onto the outside rear tire.
- To increase front tire grip (to reduce understeer), allow the inside rear tire to become more unweighted.

To get the most performance out of your kart in the rain, you will need to change the setup. Typical adjustments would be:

- Move the seat forward and upwards (raise it)
- Increase the toe-out on the front wheels

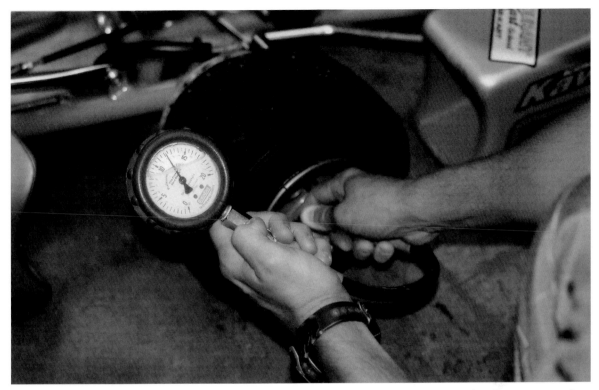

Altering tire pressures is the most common chassis-tuning tool. Make sure you are using the same good-quality, consistently accurate pressure gauge each time you check and adjust your tires. Imagine what would happen if you checked the pressures with two different gauges that didn't agree with each other.

• Widen the front track as much as possible
• Narrow the rear track

These are very general rules (and not all the possible options, either), and you will need to do some testing to determine what works for you and your kart.

Tires

We began this book by stating that the most important component of the kart is its tires. It stands to reason, then, that they are a critical tool in tuning the handling of the kart.

Your primary option in tuning the chassis with the tires is adjusting the tire pressure. The good news is that tire pressures can have a great effect on the kart's handling characteristics. Your overall goal, with most tires, is to have the pressures equal when they are hot—when you

have just come off the track. This may require setting them unevenly when they are cold, knowing that they will not heat up equally. For example, if most of the turns on a track are right-handers, the left side tires will be doing more work, and therefore will tend to heat up more. If this is the case, you would probably set the left side tires a little lower than the right side when they are cold.

If you come into the pits during a testing or practice session, you can adjust the pressures so that they are equal side to side when the tires are hot. That will also indicate to you how much you need to alter them when they are cold. For example, let's say you originally set the pressures equally when they were cold, and then when you came in with them hot, the left side tires were 2 pounds higher.

This should tell you that the next time you should set the left side tires 2 pounds lower than the right's when they are cold. That way, when hot, they should be even.

Most often, you alter the tire pressures to change the handling characteristics. To reduce the amount of understeer or oversteer, you can alter the pressures by as little as one-half a pound (most drivers cannot feel changes smaller than that). Whether to increase or decrease the pressure to control the understeer or oversteer depends on the type of tire, chassis, and your driving style. You will have to determine this for yourself in testing or practice; make changes to the tire pressures, and note the effect it has on the kart. That knowledge will help you fine-tune your kart's handling come qualifying and race time.

Often, in qualifying, to get the maximum grip for a few laps you would either raise or lower the pressures—depending on the tire. Using this approach takes some time to get used to. Do not go out in a qualifying session trying this if you have never tried it before. You will only end up going slower than ever before if you are not used to the feel of the higher or lower pressures.

You can also adjust the handling of your kart by changing the size and compound of the tires. This is way beyond the scope of this book, and maybe even most of the karters reading it. The problem is that you can really get yourself confused when you start mixing and matching different compounds. You really need to know what you are doing— or better yet, have the support of the tire manufacturer technicians.

Engine

Probably the biggest error that new karters make is not learning the basics about how to operate their karts. In their hurry to go

play, they often overlook the critical fundamentals—including how best to start their engines, fuel/oil mixtures, and how to tune and set the carburetor adjustments. Without these, they spend more time struggling to get the kart started than they do driving it. And once they get it started, with the wrong carb settings, there is a good chance that the engine will seize up ("stick").

Of course, the best way to start is simply to ask questions. Ask your engine builder, the person who owned the kart before you, or the karting shop that sold you the kart. Don't be afraid to ask questions, but do be careful whom you ask. Ask the right people.

To get the most performance out of your kart, the carb must be set properly. Be aware, though, of what appears to be conflicting advice. Two different people may give you two apparently different settings for your carb, although both settings may actually be the same. It's just that the method of adjustment or the starting point used may be different. The important thing is for you to understand the "why" and "what it does" behind the adjustments, not just "set it here and it will work."

So, in case you don't have anyone to ask advice from, following are a few rules for tuning a two-stroke engine.

Your objective in adjusting the carburetor is to find the perfect air-fuel mixture. If the mixture is too rich (that is, the engine is receiving too much fuel), the engine will not perform well. It will feel as though it is flooded when you get back on the throttle after decelerating, as it takes a second or two to clear out all the fuel and get going again— it will bog down. You may also notice more smoke coming from the exhaust when running too rich, as the engine burns off the excess fuel. Although running rich will not

Data acquisition systems are becoming more and more popular with kart racers. Here chief instructor Alan Rudolph reviews a student's performance.

physically hurt the engine (other than possibly fouling the spark plug), it will not produce its maximum power—you will be slow.

On the other hand, if the engine runs too lean (too much air and not enough fuel), you will hurt it. It will overheat, lose power, and eventually (in a very short period of time) stick—the engine will seize. What happens is that the piston and cylinder do not receive enough of a cooling effect from the fuel; they both expand until there is not enough clearance between the two; and the piston literally sticks, or seizes, to the cylinder wall.

Once an engine has begun to overheat, it is extremely difficult, if not impossible, to get it back to its normal operating temperature. If you physically feel the engine getting too hot with the right side of your body, it may be too late. It may be best to stop immediately if you want to avoid sticking the engine. If you feel the engine beginning to lose power, you may be able to save it—open up the bottom-end jet (richening the mixture) and choke the engine by physically putting your hand over the air intake.

Given the option of being too rich or too lean, it is always safer to run a bit too rich.

Changing the sprocket sizes alters the gear ratio, allowing you to optimize the engine rpm range for each track you race on. Checking the tightness of the chain, keeping it lubricated, and watching for wear are some of the most important maintenance steps.

However, the engine produces its peak power when the mixture is just right—not too rich and not too lean. To make matters more challenging, the ideal mixture is not the same at low rpm as it is at high rpm. That is why the carb has two jets: one for the top end and one for the bottom end.

The best approach is to set the carb to the engine-builder's recommendations (usually, a little on the rich side), and then go onto the track to fine-tune from there. Once the engine is warmed up, and as you are driving down a straightaway, begin to close the high-end jet slowly, until it feels as though it "cleans out." Then, just open it back up slightly, but not so much that it feels rich again.

Now, do the same with the bottom-end jet, tuning it so that it accelerates cleanly off the corners. If you close the bottom-end jet too far because it is rich coming out of the corners, you may have to richen it back up on the straightaway. It is all about finding the right balance between the two so that the kart accelerates quickly off the corners and pulls all the way to the end of the straightaways. Ideally, you want to run the engine as rich as possible without it affecting the power.

Brian Hosford makes a note of maintenance items and chassis adjustments. Always record every change you make to your kart so that you can refer back to it when you have a similar handling problem in the future. Records also make it easier to go back to your baseline setup.

Once you've found the right settings for the particular air and temperature conditions, leave them alone. Too many drivers spend way too much time fiddling with the settings. Every time they head down the straight, they are tweaking away on the mixture. What they really need to do is put that much focus on their own driving. Yes, if you are in a race or lengthy practice session where the track conditions or kart setup puts an excessive strain on the engine over a period of time, you may have to richen the setting slightly to prevent it from overheating.

Sometimes you may want to lean the engine out a bit for the start, just to maximize the engine's power—but make sure you richen it back up again or you are going to stick the engine later in the race. In wet conditions you can also lean the engine out, since there is not much worry about the engine overheating—and the fact that you are running at lower rpm necessitates leaning it out anyway. Otherwise, set it once and just drive.

When you come off the track with the jets set right, take a marker and make a line, and then count the rotations from fully closed. Make a note of the exact setting and reset them. Then, before heading back out onto the track check them again to make sure they haven't been moved. There is nothing worse than getting onto the track only to realize you have no idea where the jets are set. At that stage, your only option is to stop and reset them from scratch.

Gearing

To ensure your kart is geared correctly for a particular track, begin by asking some questions of your fellow karters with experience on that track. Your overall objective is to gear the kart so that the engine stays within its power band for the longest time.

Of course, with a direct-drive kart especially, this is going to be a compromise. After all, it is doubtful that you can keep the engine in the ideal range through the tightest corners and down the longest straight. If the track has only one slow corner and many long straights, you are probably better off leaning toward gearing it for the straights. If, on the other hand, there are a few slow corners and only one long straight, you may be better served to gear it lower, sacrificing some of the speed at the end of the straightaway.

You really have to look at what your priorities are. Is it better to accelerate quickly out of the corners, or to be fast at the end of the straight? Have the track conditions changed significantly—has it started to rain? And if you gear the kart to pull the engine's maximum rpm all the time, your engine rebuild budget will need to be a little higher than if you geared it a tooth lower.

Checklists and Record-Keeping

If you plan to keep karting for a period of time (anything beyond three or four races!), do yourself a favor and keep records of all the chassis, tire, and engine adjustments you make—not just what the settings are, but why you made them and what their effects are. Guaranteed, you will learn more and derive more enjoyment from karting if you do this. You say you are just karting for fun, and don't want to take it all that seriously? Even more reason, then, to keep records. More karters have become frustrated and quit because of a lack of progress than just about anything else (with the possible exception of the rising costs).

And speaking of costs, if you keep records of the changes you have made, and checklists of the things you need to do to prepare the kart, you will save money. Frequently, the savings are huge. A lot of costly crashes and engine failures are a result of lack of preparation. And that lack of preparation is usually a lack of planning—keeping track of what needs to be done before the next session or race.

After a brief period of using checklists to keep track of what maintenance must be done on a regular basis, you will identify areas that need more attention and others that require less attention. This is one of the main reasons keeping records and checklists can save you some serious money.

Keeping records and using checklists does not add any time to your karting outing. In fact, it usually saves time by allowing you to focus on the important things. The bottom line, though, is that it will make karting more relaxing and enjoyable—and you will learn more, faster.

Whether your goal is to race karts for the rest of your life, or use them as a springboard to a career racing cars, kart racing offers a tremendous challenge and learning experience—not to mention fun! My main wish is that you get as much out of kart racing as I have out of my racing career. Be safe, drive fast, and have fun. See you at the race track.

Index